THE END OF

LIBRARIES

'I do not propose to go into the history of ignoring users, since there is not time to give an account of librarianship from its beginnings.'

— Maurice Line

'Any concept of a library that begins with books on shelves is sure to encounter trouble.'

— J C R Licklider

'We seem to be fast coming to the day when, unless it is afforded the most expert sort of bibliographical service possible, civilization may die of suffocation, choked in its own plethora of print.'

— Fremont Rider

'We are already very close to the day in which a great science library could exist in a space less than 10 feet square.'

— F W Lancaster

'While you were watching television, the book died.' *— A R Turnbull*

'Librarianship of the database is coming.' *— P R Lewis*

THE END OF

LIBRARIES

JAMES THOMPSON

LIBRARIAN
University of Reading

CLIVE BINGLEY LONDON

By the same author:

AN INTRODUCTION TO UNIVERSITY LIBRARY ADMINISTRATION
(3rd ed, 1979)

LIBRARY POWER

A HISTORY OF THE PRINCIPLES OF LIBRARIANSHIP

UNIVERSITY LIBRARY HISTORY
(Editor)

Copyright © James Thompson 1982

Published by Clive Bingley Limited, 16 Pembridge Road, London W11 3HL, and printed and bound in England by Redwood Burn Limited, Trowbridge, Wiltshire.

First published 1982

British Library Cataloguing in Publication Data

Thompson, James, *1932-*
    The end of libraries.
    1. Libraries
    I. Title
            025.56   Z711.2
            ISBN 0-85157-349-5

Typeset by Allset in 10 on 12 point Press Roman

CONTENTS

5

Chapter 1

THE UNUSABLE LIBRARY

The concept of the unusable library is more familiar to library users than to librarians. For a start most libraries are far too large for ready consultation. Furthermore they seem to the majority of their users to store books 'in such a way that no one can find them without several years' training'.[1] Likewise the catalogues provided to these enormous collections appear to be essentially inventories for the custodians rather than finding aids designed for the users. 'I do not propose to go into the history of ignoring users', Maurice Line once remarked to a conference of librarians, 'since there is not time to give an account of librarianship from its beginnings'.[2]

The situation is further compounded by the contradictions in the nature of the book itself as a means of recording knowledge. The printed page as such is a superb method of displaying information. It affords, in the words of J C R Licklider,[3] 'enough resolution to meet the eye's demand. It presents enough information to occupy the reader for a convenient quantum of time. It offers great flexibility of font and format. It lets the reader control the mode and rate of inspection. It is small, light, movable, cuttable, clippable, pastable, replicable, disposable, and inexpensive'.

However, as Licklider goes on to explain, once printed pages are bound together to make books or journals most of the display features of the individual pages are diminished or destroyed. If these same bound books and journals are then housed by the million in libraries, the resultant arrangement is bound to become more and more unusable as libraries continue to grow. 'Any concept of a library that begins with books on shelves,' Licklider declares, 'is sure to encounter trouble'.

Some twenty years previously, in the nineteen-forties, Fremont Rider[4] had arrived at precisely the same conclusion. The starting-point for Rider was his concern with library growth. He calculated that over a period of three centuries, without substantial deviation either

7

upwards or downwards, American research libraries had on average doubled in size every sixteen years. Taking Yale as a specific example, he found that it had grown from 1,000 volumes in the early part of the eighteenth century, to 2,748,000 volumes in 1938, and would by the year 2040 reach 200,000,000 volumes. He also calculated that if in 1938 Yale needed 80 miles of shelving, a card catalogue of some 10,000 drawers and a staff of over 200 (half of whom would be involved in cataloguing), in 2040 Yale would have to have 6,000 miles of shelving, 750,000 catalogue drawers occupying 8 acres of floor space, and 6,000 cataloguing staff.

This was the impending impasse to which Rider addressed himself. He argued that 'no emendations in present library method alone were going to provide a sufficient solution', and that it was no longer possible to accept as axiomatic such assumptions and dicta as: libraries are collections of books, books are stored on shelves, library materials have to be catalogued, catalogues have to be made on cards, books must be arranged by their class-marks. 'Libraries are great complexes of tiny items,' he concluded, 'items which it is almost impossible to handle in any way *en bloc* because each one, tiny though it is, is highly individualized and demands equally individualistic treatment. It is this combination of enormous mass and extreme individualization of detail that has gone far to make the problem so difficult to solve'.

Libraries have however remained locked in their growth spiral. According to figures issued by the Association of Research Libraries, Yale reached 7,246,195 volumes in 1978-79. In the same year the libraries of the University of California contained amongst them 14,837,130 volumes; and the Library of Congress just on its own held 18,949,850 volumes. A recent President of the British Library Association, in an address appropriately called *Information, the 'unscarce' resource*,[5] reported another staggering statistic from America: that in the mid-seventies the 32,000 public, academic and special libraries, and the 75,000 school libraries in that affluent country owned between them 1,300 million volumes. Even in the context of the very much more modest British economy, the Education, Science and Arts Committee of the House of Commons learned in Session 1979-80[6] that the total available stock of books in United Kingdom libraries is of the order of 250 million volumes.

From the point of view of the library user it is not possible to justify the acquisition by libraries of this enormous mass of material. Not only is there concrete evidence in the United Kingdom that for some years

8

the number of books being borrowed from our ever-increasing public libraries is falling, but in America there have been several studies of the patterns of the use of books in research libraries which demonstrate a very large discrepancy between the amount of material which libraries acquire and the amount which users use. One of the most recent of these studies, that conducted at the University of Pittsburgh[7] by a team led by Professor Allen Kent, reveals that only 56-60% of the books added to the Pittsburgh library collections in any one year ever circulate. 40% are never used at all. Professor Kent comments: 'This suggests that a combination of collection size and use is necessary to measure library effectiveness'.

What makes the Pittsburgh study all the more striking is the simple fact that it is an assessment of a library system in the type of setting which, perhaps above all others, should be the most conducive to library use. The University of Pittsburgh is a large, research-orientated institution, covering a wide range of subject disciplines, with a student population in excess of 22,000 and a teaching staff of over 2,000. The library's clientele is a captive one: motivated, purposive, committed. Library use in such an academic environment is virtually obligatory. Why therefore, asks Professor Kent, are 40% of Pittsburgh's books never used?

One of his conclusions is that libraries must re-examine their acquisition policies. If the justification for a level of acquisition almost twice the level of measurable current use is some attempt at completeness, this is damned at the outset of Professor Kent's study. He estimates that since the invention of printing some 30 million unique titles have been published. Not even the world's largest library, the Library of Congress, approaches anywhere near 30 million titles, and only a very limited number of libraries indeed contain more than 5% of them.

If the justification is that a library should aim to cater for future, as well as current needs, Professor Kent's answer is a blunt one: 'There is no objective way to forecast future needs, and consequently there is no objective way to make acquisition decisions with the certain knowledge that what is acquired will be used'. The argument is further eroded by the findings of an earlier library use study. In the nineteen-sixties Fussler and Simon[8] established that past use was the best predictor of future use: that is, the forty or so per cent of the research library collection which is not used currently is not likely to be used in the future either.

It is ironic that in recent decades libraries have also been alarmed to discover that the material which they are supposedly storing for the future is physically disintegrating in their care. Books do not last forever. Much of today's printed material will not survive to be available for future generations: certainly not newspapers, for example, nor mass-produced paperbacks. There is no hope for the truly permanent retention of printed matter unless libraries embark on a massive conservation programme at huge cost. A more realistic programme is the transformation of print on paper into some other form. Currently the library user is witnessing the large-scale substitution of microfilm and microfiche versions for older and less durable works. In the context of the concept of the unusable library the ultimate irony is that after forty years there is still little sign that microform is becoming more acceptable as a device for the acquisition of information by the general reader.[9]

The sheer size of the book and other collections is only the first of the barriers encountered by library users. The next is how the books are arranged. For most library users this is still the main determinant as to whether or not they find what they need. The majority of libraries employ one or other of the two main general book classification schemes: the Dewey Decimal system, or the Library of Congress system. Dewey was devised in the 1870s, the age of horse transport and gas lighting (if not oil-lamps). Continuous revision has not affected its essentially nineteenth century character, nor has the patching in of Einstein and Freud, telephones and automobiles, computers and television, nuclear fission and space flight. The Library of Congress system, likewise, belongs to the turn of the century.

The inadequacies and vagaries of these two outdated schemes have bewildered and frustrated generations of library users. Libraries are, however, powerless to relinquish them. Such is the size of present-day book collections that the costs of reclassification cannot be contemplated. It is axiomatic in traditional librarianship that the cost of processing a book for library use — acquiring it, cataloguing it, classifying it — is about the same as the cost of buying it in the first place. No major library can realistically contemplate the financial outlay which a thoroughgoing reclassification programme would require. The chances of the Library of Congress in Washington reclassifying its 19 million volumes are nil. Moreover, the prevailing international systems producing current bibliographic records are also locked into these two schemes, and are therefore committed to promoting and endorsing their continuance. More modern classification schemes have been devised, and could be devised: but they can never be implemented to any significant extent.

10

But quite apart from the defects of existing classification schemes as such, there is the more radical problem referred to earlier: the nature of the book itself. A book classification can never be more than a method of arranging books as individual items according to their broad subject matter in some kind of comprehensible sequence. A book however need not be restricted in coverage to any one subject or any one aspect of a subject. Nevertheless it can occupy only one place on one shelf. Likewise there will always exist a very real distinction between subject matter, in the simple classificatory sense, and actual use. To give an example: suppose a library user is seeking a picture of factory conditions at the height of the Industrial Revolution in Britain. Such a picture might be found in books on the Industrial Revolution; or on social history; or on labour history; or on industrial architecture; or in a descriptive study of an industrial town.

A book is a comparatively sophisticated device. In its own right it is adequately usable. It has its own internal apparatus: contents list, list of illustrations, chapter and section headings, list of references, index. But it is altogether too individual an item for *en bloc* classification (to hark back to Fremont Rider's argument).

Libraries have attempted, quite unsuccessfully, to palliate users' difficulties first by introducing open access arrangements, and subsequently by setting up elaborate user education programmes. It is perhaps necessary to explain that historically one of the longest traditions in librarianship has been to deny users direct access to the book collections. It was well into the twentieth century before such access became the general rule. The practical effect of the concession however was to ·throw the library user even more on his own resources. The resultant need for instruction in library use led in turn to an international multiplicity of elaborate and expensive user education programmes, the majority of them embarrassingly inept.

Oldman and Wills[10] have investigated in some depth the lack of what they call 'user orientation' in libraries. Libraries plainly operate on the basis that the onus is on the user to learn how to use the system. User failure is to be overcome not by system reforms but by teaching the user the mysteries of librarianship. 'When users complain about the physical scatter of their subject in their library, the response often as not will be: that is how Dewey operates. What perhaps should be developed is *librarian's education* programmes, not user education programmes. Supermarket managers who learn that their customers cannot find an in-stock product on their shelves blame themselves not their customers. They seek to manage their store to reduce such difficulties.'

In defending the complexities of their book arrangements libraries are often driven to resort to the argument that the only true key to a library is its catalogue. But the other major conclusion of Professor Allen Kent's Pittsburgh study was that the effectiveness of the card catalogue had to be in doubt in the light of the evidence that only 56-60% of the Pittsburgh collections were used. He comments that if it can be shown that the card catalogue does not allow reasonable access to the book collections, then new approaches to bibliographic access would be in order.

Professor Kent's mildly expressed doubts about library catalogues would be echoed rather more strongly by the majority of library users. The size and complexity of author catalogues, and the rules employed by cataloguers for the choice of headings and for filing, are not readily comprehended. Moreover the dedication of libraries to author catalogues as such must in itself strike many users as unhelpful. If users do remember a particular work it is just as likely (perhaps even more likely) that it will be the title rather than the author they will remember. More importantly, a subject approach is what the majority of library users employ in seeking information. Libraries over the decades have nevertheless been very slow to introduce subject catalogues. When subject catalogues did become common, the form most favoured by libraries was the classified catalogue. Classified catalogues are almost toally unused by library users: they are the ultimate illustration of the concept of the unusable library. By contrast, libraries which have offered a form of alphabetical subject catalogue — familiar to users, as a dictionary or an encyclopedia is — have been surprised at the high level of use.

Both J C R Licklider and Fremont Rider queried the effectiveness of library catalogues, but from a very much more radical stance. Rider commented: 'We seem to be fast coming to the day when, unless it is afforded the most expert sort of bibliographical service possible, civilization may die of suffocation, choked in its own plethora of print'. His analysis of the situation was that the basic trouble stemmed from the traditional viewpoint in libraries that catalogue problems and book storage problems were separate problems. His solution was to suggest that a library's catalogue should be in the form of microcards: that is, on one side of the card would be the catalogue entry, as in a conventional catalogue: but that on the other would be the text of the book itself, reproduced micrographically. Rider's solution was conceptually correct; it failed to materialize because the technological method he proposed (the only one available to him in the nineteen-forties) was not a pre-emptive one.

Licklider went much further than Rider, focusing his analysis on what he described as the 'passiveness' of the printed page. He pointed out that 'when information is stored in books, there is no practical way to transfer the information from the store to the user without physically moving the book or the reader or both'; and he argued that what was needed was 'a device that will make it easy to transmit information without transporting material, and that will not only present information to people but also process it for them, following procedures they specify, apply, monitor, and, if necessary, revise and reapply'. The solution he suggested was to substitute for the traditional combination of catalogues and books a 'meld of library and computer'. Again conceptually his analysis cannot be contested. In this instance though, the technology proposed — the computer — *is* pre-emptive.

By pre-emptive is meant that such are the possibilities offered that there can be no option but to embrace them: just as after the invention of the internal combustion engine there could be no long-term future for the horse-and-cart. As has been argued, traditionally organized libraries have reached an impasse in terms of usability: they are too large, they are defectively and anachronistically arranged, and the principal finding aid they offer users — the card catalogue — is largely ineffectual.

But not only is there this organizational impasse which has made libraries increasingly unusable. There is also looming an economic impasse which will make them financially insupportable. There have been fiscal difficulties for libraries in the United States for the last ten or more years: Herbert S White[11] wrote recently that libraries, particularly academic libraries, have been playing a losing game with their materials budgets for quite some time now. Their financial environment has undergone a drastic change: 'Increasing publication rates, skyrocketing inflation, and a general de-emphasis on education because of societal priorities viewed as more pressing, have all combined to make it impossible for library managers to continue to buy everything which appears to be value or interest'. No longer is it possible to pursue acquisition policies 'designed to produce on each campus the self-contained Alexandrian library'. White's advice to libraries is the advice he himself received from a tennis coach in his college days: always change a losing game. Since libraries are about to lose anyway, any alteration in strategy can do no harm.

In the United Kingdom the financial climate for libraries is even worse. Economic recession and political policy are reducing funds for all types of library. An exemplification of the official discouragement of library growth was the Atkinson Report,[12] the report of a Working Party of the University Grants Committee which proposed a 'new concept' of the way in which a library might work. Instead of what it regarded as the traditional concept of indefinite accumulation, the Working Party put forward the concept of a 'self-renewing' library, in which the intake of new accessions would be 'relieved' or offset by the withdrawal of obsolete or unconsulted materials to other stores. Libraries would be of limited size, based primarily on student numbers. While the recommendations of this report not surprisingly produced a hostile reaction from academic libraries, its underlying governmental message was unmistakeable.

The overall situation in both countries, and indeed in all of the developed world, was succinctly described in an issue of *Business weekly* (31 March 1981) thus: 'Beset on the one hand by the soaring costs of energy, buildings, and published material, and on the other by onrushing technology that threatens ultimately to make the printed word obsolete, the library is going through a major identity crisis that is forcing dramatic changes in how it operates'.

The pressure on traditionally organized libraries to change their game, to adopt on behalf of their users an over-riding concept of usability, is now intense. As far back as 1945, Dr Vannevar Bush[13] reflected that Mendel's work on the laws of genetics was lost to the world for a generation because his publication did not reach the few who were capable of grasping and extending it; but more worrying still, the level of publication in modern times had been extended far beyond our ability to make real use of the record. 'The summation of human experience', he wrote, 'is being expanded at a prodigious rate, and the means we use for threading through the consequent maze to the momentarily important item is the same as was used in the days of square-rigged ships'.

In similar vein, in the United Kingdom in 1948, the Royal Society held a Scientific Information Conference[14] to air the growing difficulties of scientists in relation to their information needs. The problem was summed up in the address by Sir Henry Tizard: 'We have already had some figures about the spate of scientific papers. I think it is quite
14

safe to say that in the whole world there are one million published every year. We have got to the stage now that we pour out information that is not used, because it is inaccessible'.

In March 1981 the Library Association of Great Britain issued a draft report on the impact of new technology in libraries and information centres and it too, by way of a warning to traditionalists, recounted a little piece of past history: 'The period 1920-1960 saw the development of the professional research worker. Most libraries of the time were book based. To keep up to date however the research worker required reports of other research more current than that generally reported in books, mostly journal articles and reports of one kind or another. The library profession failed to respond adequately to the needs of this group which eventually broke away from the main body, formed its own organization and developed its own techniques for handling this different form of material'.

Libraries were given an even more contemporaneous warning by Maurice Line[15] at a recent conference on information provision. 'If some libraries and their staffs do not become rather more user-friendly', he commented, 'the friends they have may desert them for computer terminals, which may have their limitations but may also have fewer user-hostile elements'.

Libraries must change because they — or, at least, *what they represent* — are too important to society. They are mankind's memory. When man first recorded information by means of incisions on clay tablets, 'the revolution caused by the sharing of experience and the spread of knowledge had begun. Today, our libraries, the descendants of those mud tablets, can be regarded as immense communal brains, memorizing far more than any one human brain could hold. When man began to use physical objects to convey experience to generations unborn, then a new and immensely important threshold had been crossed. His pictographs and his writings, his books, microfilm and computer tapes can be seen as extra-corporeal DNA, adjuncts to our genetical inheritance as important and influential in determining the way we behave as the chromosomes in our tissues are in determining the physical shape of our bodies. It was this accumulated wisdom that eventually enabled us to devise ways of escaping the dictates of the environment. Our knowledge of agricultural techniques and mechanical devices, of medicine and engineering, of mathematics and space travel, all depends on stored experience. Cut off from our libraries and all they represent and marooned on a desert island,

15

any one of us would be quickly reduced to the life of a hunter gatherer'.[16]

This line of progression over a period of three thousand years — from clay tablet to papyrus roll, from parchment manuscript through five hundred years of the printed book — has begun to founder. Such is the present size of the library-held communal brain, and so unusable has the traditional system now become, that the emergence in recent years of a new technology with an infinitely superior potential to store and retrieve knowledge must be accepted as pre-emptive. Libraries cannot continue as they are. In evolutionary terms the obvious analogy is with the spectacularly sudden extinction of the dinosaurs.

References

1 Cornford, F M *Microcosmographia academica*. 1908.

2 Line, Maurice B *Ignoring the user: how, when and why*. The nationwide provision and use of information: Aslib/IIS/LA Joint Conference, Sheffield, September 1980.

3 Licklider, J C R *Libraries of the future*. Cambridge, Mass., MIT Press, 1965.

4 Rider, Fremont *The scholar and the future of the research library*. New York, Hadham Press, 1944.

5 Saunders, W L *Information, the 'unscarce' resource*. The nationwide provision and use of information: Aslib/IIS/LA Joint Conference, Sheffield, September 1980.

6 House of Commons *Fourth report from the Education, Science and Arts Committee, Session 1979-80*. London, HMSO, 1980.

7 *Use of library materials: the University of Pittsburgh study*. New York, Marcel Dekker, 1979.

8 Fussler, Herman J *and* Simon, Julian L *Patterns in the use of books in large research libraries*. Chicago, University of Chicago Press, 1969.

9 Meadows, Arthur Jack *New technology developments in the communication of research during the 1980s*. Leicester, Primary Communications Research Centre, University of Leicester, 1980.

10 Oldman, Christine *and* Wills, Gordon *A re-appraisal of academic librarianship*. Bradford, MCB Publications, 1978.

11 White, Herbert S 'Bjorn Borg and the library materials budget' *Information and library manager*, 1 (1), June 1981.

12 University Grants Committee *Capital provision for university libraries: report of a Working Party*. London, HMSO, 1976.

16

13 Bush, Vannevar 'As we may think' *The Atlantic monthly*, July, 1945.

14 Royal Society Scientific Information Conference, 21 June-2 July 1948: *Report and papers submitted*. London, Royal Society, 1948.

15 Line, Maurice B, *op. cit.*, 2.

16 Attenborough, David *Life on earth*. London, Collins, 1979.

Chapter 2

THE PRE-EMPTIVE TECHNOLOGY

The pre-emptive technology is the potent combination of computers, in which information can be stored and processed, and telecommunications, by means of which information can be transmitted to anybody anywhere in the world. Libraries need not be visited (and libraries, especially comprehensive or specialist libraries, are not everywhere available); card catalogues need not be consulted (even assuming that they could ever have been made truly effective); shelves need not be searched (again assuming items in libraries are always readily findable); and books need not be scanned (an exercise which is time-consuming even for the expert and experienced).

This interconnection between computers and telecommunications was christened 'telematics' by Simon Nora and Alain Minc, the authors of a report (first published in 1978) to the President of France, on the computerization of society. Introducing the English translation of the report,[1] Daniel Bell observes that the idea has been in the air for a long time and recalls other similar neologisms: 'compunications', coined by Anthony Oettinger of Harvard to describe the merger of computers, telephone and television into a new kind of digital code, a single yet differentiated system that allows for the transmission of data or inter-action between persons or computers speaking to computers, through telephone lines, cables, microwave relays, or satellites; and 'domonetics', coined by Allan Kiron, a word derived from domicile, nexus, and electronics, to indicate the change in living patterns that the decentralization of work would make possible. More recent coinages include those used by Alvin Toffler,[2] who talks of 'telecommunity' (to describe the possibilities offered by computers and telecommunications for the strengthening of bonds and relationships in the home and the community), the 'electronic cottage' (whereby computers and telecommunications will make it possible for large numbers of people to give up commuting and instead work at home or in nearby neighbourhood
18

centres), and the 'info-sphere' (the gradual substitution of communications for transportation).

Whichever term or terms may prevail, however, what is being expressed is an innovation that will transform society in the way railroads and electricity did in the nineteenth century. Nora and Minc comment that while the computer is not the only technological innovation of recent years it does constitute the common factor that speeds the development of all the others. Since it is responsible for the upheaval in the processing and storage of data it is bound to alter 'the entire nervous system of social organization'. Computer data processing is moreover no longer expensive. The miniaturization and low cost of electronic components now means that a microprocessor only a few millimetres wide has the same processing capability as a computer of ten or fifteen years ago which occupied an entire room. By way of vivid illustration Nora and Minc point out that if the price of a Rolls Royce had evolved in comparable fashion, the most luxurious model would cost one franc today. Released from the burden of concern over component costs, manufacturers are now able to focus their efforts on improving the usability and accessiblity of data processing systems.

Government interest in the new pre-emptive technology has not of course been confined only to France. In the United Kingdom there have been two reports: one from the Education, Science and Arts Committee of the House of Commons (July 1980),[3] and one from the Advisory Council for Applied Research and Development of the Cabinet Office (September 1980).[4]

The purpose of the former was to enquire into the implications of electronic data processing and transmission, in relation to the development of library services. One of its first findings was that libraries could not be studied in isolation from the many other agencies in 'the network of information'. Dependence on accessibility of information was common to industry, commerce, public administration, and to every individual. 'Modern technology', observed the report, 'is now offering new forms of information storage and retrieval. There are three key components of the new technology. First, new ways to store information compactly and cheaply — photographic microforms of various kinds, magnetic storage on tapes and discs, optical storage and video discs, holographic memories. Second, new mechanisms to manipulate, scan and search such stored records — the large-scale computer, the minicomputer, the microprocessor and related devices. Third, new facilities for cheap and rapid transmission of information over long distances — telecommunication systems and networks'.

In its evidence to the Committee, the British Library stated that 'it seems probable there will be a progressive movement towards a situation where very large quantities of information, including complete texts of reports, journals and other publications, can be stored cheaply and compactly by electronic means, and interrogated, retrieved, transmitted and made available rapidly and economically in a variety of forms'; while Aslib noted that 'on a small seven-inch disc we can expect a storage of half a million pages . . . they can be stored in libraries all round the country . . . if the content needs to be dispatched quickly it can go overnight on uncrowded telephone lines'.

The ACARD report was the outcome of a Working Group set up especially to look at the whole subject of 'information technology' in order to identify the likely directions of development, and existing constraints on development and application in the United Kingdom. The stimulus had come from a previous ACARD report, on technological change, which had singled out information technology as possibly the area of application with the greatest potential for creating employment, suggesting that the United Kingdom had advantages — for example, the international use of the English language — which should enable it to gain a significant share of the world market for information services and associated products.

The ACARD report is significant in that it displays no interest whatsoever in libraries nor in the concerns of libraries. Unlike the report of the Education, Science and Arts Committee it does not even attempt to build a bridge between mankind's traditional extension of human memory — libraries — and the prospect of a universal electronic memory. It demonstrates in its own right, with powerful clarity, the truly pre-emptive nature of the new technology.

The report states that the principal foundation for modern information technology has been the development of microelectronics, which makes possible small, low cost, reliable equipment which can perform complex operations on digitally encoded data. Increasingly all types of information are being converted to digital form because of the ease with which such data can be handled and transmitted. The report explains that information handling comprises five stages — input, processing, storage, transmission and output — and that the systems employed are made up of equipment (hardware) and, most importantly, logical programs (software) which control the operation of both individual pieces of equipment and of the systems as a whole.

Input, the first stage, can be by means of keyboard, telephone dial and keypad, optical character recognition, special writing pads, voice recognition and systems now being developed which will extract features from visual images such as photographs and television pictures. Processing, of course, is by computer: local processing by small computers, with large computers for maintaining and manipulating large banks of data. All information which until the present time has been stored in words, figures, graphs, charts and pictures, can now be translated into sequences of binary digits (bits) — that is, ones and zeros. The resulting digital data can be stored in electronic memories which technologically continue to grow in capacity and decrease in real cost. Other storage devices are being developed with a similar potential: magnetic 'bubble' memories, and video discs, for example.

Transmission can be by cable, radio frequency and satellite. A new development here is transmission over optical fibres, opening up the possibility of carrying very large quantities of information for a variety of uses, relieving existing congested cross-city cable routes and providing low cost trunk and local distribution networks for telephones, data transmission, television and videophones. The continuing reduction in the cost of small ground terminals for receiving signals from satellites has also, the report notes, begun to make direct communication between two points via satellite economical, as well as reducing dependence on cable and terrestrial radio systems. Output can be by way of a visual display unit, or a printer. Visual display units in the form of a cathode ray tube (as in a television set) can use colour and show both text and graphical information. The report predicts the likely development of a flat screen display, based not on a cathode ray tube but on a thin sheet of light-emitting material or a fine grid of light-emitting devices. Printers are becoming faster and quieter. There is also the prospect of output in the form of voice synthesizers, likely to be important in personal voice communication systems, including the instruction of users in the use of new facilities.

In the ACARD Working Group's view the outcome of all of these developments in information technology will be a marked increase in the quantity of rapidly accessible information and in the ability to manipulate it. As printing and distribution costs rise and communications and computing costs fall, these systems 'may come to replace some paper publications'. In office work, within the next ten years, 'it may be cheaper to capture information and to file, copy and transmit it electronically, than to perform the same functions on paper'. Numerous

21

applications are already in evidence in public administration (social security records, payroll calculations, revenue collection, defence logistics, motorway maintenance, police files); retailing (for example, the now familiar systems in shops based on the use of bar codes); insurance, banking and finance; communications and transport (seat reservation systems have been commonplace for years now); printing and publishing; health services; legal services; and education.

The final words of the ACARD Working Group merit quotation in full: 'Our concluding note, in line with the central theme of this report, is that Government, industry, commerce, trade unions and the professions must take the new developments in information handling very seriously. They will affect working arrangements, management systems and personal life. They offer great commercial opportunities for this country if successfully exploited. It will be necessary to examine the changes in management organization and techniques which are necessary to make best use of information technology. The Civil Service, local government, and industrial and commercial managements are frequently aware of the systems which are available but are sometimes slow in adjusting their method of working to make effective use of them. It is essential to start not from the way that tasks are tackled with present methods but to examine the true tasks to be performed and how they can best be undertaken with the aid of the new technology'.

The key phrase is plainly 'the true tasks'. Libraries have been traditionally slow to perceive their true tasks. The outcome has been the unusable library: mankind's memory uncritically amassed, esoterically arranged and inventoried, and only grudgingly accessible. As Oldman and Wills observed,[5] librarians, 'like managers of numerous less than successful enterprises,' so often display a 'product orientation' (that is, a preoccupation with books and records as such) as opposed to a 'user orientation'. Likewise, and more seriously, as the present author has previously argued,[6] they have consistently disregarded the true source of their power: that libraries have been the storehouses of knowledge and the repositories of man's achievements and discoveries, conserving and transmitting his culture, underpinning his education, featuring significantly in his economic welfare, and relating crucially to all other intellectual, artistic and creative activities. They have been the instruments of social and political change and, as the guardians of the freedom of thought, the bastions of man's liberty.

Just as the Nora and Minc report reflected government interest in

France in the implications of the new information technology, and the House of Commons and ACARD reports government interest in the United Kingdom, in the United States also there has been a similar high-level concern, which culminated in the White House Conference on Libraries and Information Services convened by President Carter in November 1979. Daniel Bell, in his introduction to the Nora and Minc report, referred to the 'quiet debate' which has been going on in America for some years. At the time he was writing, June 1979, he reported that there were before the 96th Congress no less than three bills to modify the Communications Act of 1939, which if passed would open up the telecommunications field to more competition and give the market a more important voice in shaping the development of 'compunications'.

American involvement in the new technology goes back to the 1950s, when computers were first applied to information retrieval. In the following decade a number of major systems were developed in the United States, notably by the Defense Documentation Center (then known as the Armed Services Technical Information Agency), the National Aeronautics and Space Administration (NASA), and the National Library of Medicine. F W Lancaster worked on both the first and last of these, and he has recounted[7] how he became initially interested in the possibilities of paperless information systems in 1972 when he discovered that the defence-intelligence community in the United States was already moving very rapidly towards fully electronic systems. He was able to see both the need for and the feasibility of paperless systems for the dissemination, storage and retrieval of intelligence information, just as Nora and Minc subsequently predicted the replacement in business and commerce of much of our 'paper economy' by an electronic transfer system.

Lancaster went on to consider the wider applicability of paperless systems and arrived at the conclusion that within the context of scientific and technical communication, not only were they feasible, but inevitable. For him the evidence was overwhelming that society was moving to a largely paperless environment, in a kind of natural evolutionary process.

He argues that simple economic necessity will not permit the communication system in science to survive indefinitely in its paper-based form. Labour resources are both costly and finite, and manual productivity as such cannot be substantially improved beyond a certain point. Conventional approaches to the publication and distribution of

23

scientific information are reaching the point where they will be unable to cope with a continued exponential growth of the literature. Primary publications (that is, principally articles in journals) and secondary publications (abstracting and indexing services) are already pricing themselves out of the market. Most of the major secondary publications are now too expensive for the individual subscriber, and are to be found only in institutions (mainly libraries). Even then, they have begun to be priced beyond the resources of the smaller institutions and soon will be afforded only by the larger, wealthier ones. Primary publication is similarly threatened: Lancaster predicts (and corroborative evidence is abundant on both sides of the Atlantic) that the printed science journal in conventional form is likely soon to be beyond the financial resources of the individual scientist so that, eventually, science journals also will be found only in libraries.

He concludes therefore that if we persist in conventional methods of information handling, science literature can only become progressively less accessible to the science community. Computer processing – the pre-emptive technology – must prevail. He calculates that at current prices it could cost a six-figure sum annually for the privilege of having on the shelves of a library a fairly comprehensive collection of secondary publications in science. A better service, both in economic and operational terms, could be offered in the form of on-line terminals to a range of computerized databases. 'We are already very close to the day', he declares, 'in which a great science library could exist in a space less than 10 feet square'.

More important, in the light of the arguments underlying the first chapter of the present work, is recognition of the fact that 'on-line access provides search capabilities that are a great improvement over the search capabilities of the printed tool'. Increasingly also, a number of specialized information sources exist only in machine-readable form. They are accessible in the electronic world but not in the world of paper. Lancaster believes that by the year 2000 formal communication in science and technology will be almost exclusively electronic.

The achievements of the intelligence community in the implementation of paperless systems do however point to much more than the application of such systems in the scientific and technical community. As described by Lancaster, the model system sought for intelligence work was to provide each analyst, through his own terminal, with on-line receipt of mail, with on-line access to his own files, branch files, Agency files and even outside databases such as the *New York*

Times Information Bank: the concept of a 'widening horizons' approach to an intelligence search.

Such a model echoes, as Lancaster was himself aware, the concept put forward in the nineteen-forties by Vannevar Bush. Bush conceived the notion of a device for individual use, a sort of mechanized private file and library. He coined a name for it, 'Memex', and his remarkable description merits quotation in full:

'A memex is a device in which an individual stores all his books, records, and communications, and which is mechanized so that it may be consulted with exceeding speed and flexibility. It is an enlarged intimate supplement to his memory.

'It consists of a desk, and while it can presumably be operated from a distance, it is primarily the piece of furniture at which he works. On the top are slanting translucent screens, on which material can be projected for convenient reading. There is a keyboard, and sets of buttons and levers. Otherwise it looks like an ordinary desk.

'In one end is the stored material. The matter of bulk is well taken care of by improved microfilm. Only a small part of the interior of the memex is devoted to storage, the rest to mechanism. Yet if the user inserted 5,000 pages of material a day it would take him hundreds of years to fill the repository, so he can be profligate and enter material freely.

'Most of the memex contents are purchased on microfilm ready for insertion. Books of all sorts, pictures, current periodicals, newspapers, are thus obtained and dropped into place. Business correspondence takes the same path. And there is provision for direct entry. On the top of the memex is a transparent platen. On this are placed longhand notes, photographs, memoranda, all sorts of things. When one is in place, the depression of a lever causes it to be photographed on to the next blank space in a section of the memex film, dry photography being employed.

'There is, of course, provision for consultation of the record by the usual scheme of indexing. If the user wishes to consult a certain book, he taps its code on the keyboard, and the title page of the book promptly appears before him, projected on to one of his viewing positions. Frequently used codes are mnemonic, so that he seldom consults his code book; but when he does, a single tap of a key projects it for his use. Moreover, he has supplemental levers. On deflecting one of these levers to the right he runs through the book before him, each page in turn being projected at a speed which just allows a recognizing glance at each. If he deflects if further to the right, he steps through the book 10 pages at a time; still further at 100 pages at a time. Deflection to the left gives him the same control backwards.

'A special button transfers him immediately to the first page of the index. Any given book of his library can thus be called up and consulted with far greater facility than if it were taken from a shelf. As he has several projection positions, he can leave one item in position while he calls up another. He can add marginal notes and comments, taking advantage of one possible type of dry photography, and it could even be arranged so that he can do this by a stylus scheme, . . . just as though he had the physical page before him.'

What was important from Bush's point of view was not what he called the 'mechanisms and gadgetry' (which indeed in the event would now be very different), but first the facility to have immediately to hand all the information *he* required, and secondly that access to that information was by personal association. He wished to be freed from the obligation to penetrate the obscurities of enormous general libraries ('the matter of selection' is his phrase), and not to have to endure the constrictions which result from 'the artificiality of systems of indexing'. He argued that the human mind does not file alphabetically or numerically, nor trace down from subclass to subclass, nor follow mutual trails singly and in isolation. It works by association: with one item in its grasp, it snaps instantly to the next that is suggested by the train of thought.

The problem with libraries is that in an absolute sense they can never be convenient. Convenience for an individual seeking information is to have that information available or delivered where he is: in his office, in his laboratory, in his home. Bush's 'Memex' is the ideal conceptual model as far as the individual user is concerned. The preemptive nature of the new technology is not merely that it has the possibility to store a vast amount of data more compactly and more economically, nor that it can process and retrieve that data more effectively than any of the traditional library systems, but that because it is a combination of computerization and telecommunications, it can achieve an unmatchable level of convenience.

A further pre-emptive element in the new systems is that they are dynamic. Bush argues that if a record is to be useful to science, it must be continuously extended, it must be stored, and above all it must be consulted. Libraries can certainly store records, though with increasing

26

difficulty in economic terms, and completely passively in the sense of a largely uncritical accumulation. Accumulation does not however meet the criterion of continuous extension: whole areas of libraries fade from use as they become outdated or outmoded: but physically, they remain, often obscuring what continues to be relevant. With the preemptive technology there is built in the facility to adopt, revise, extend, reduce, delete. This of course is a derivative of ready consultation.

Bush's conceptual model of an individual's own information station is to be seen not only as the kind of target which the American intelligence community have worked towards, but for very general, widespread use also. The ACARD report referred to earlier included this comment: 'Information technology will give the individual at home a better, wider range of communications and immediate access to a far greater range of information. It will be possible to store and use personal information. Electronic mail may replace some correspondence and telephoning, and electronic means may be used for the payment of bills if ways can be found for establishing personal identity and authority, to eliminate the possibility of fraud. Information technology will enable more people to work at home, with particular benefit for those who could not otherwise find employment'.

It would now be possible, for example, to develop for individual farmers an agricultural information system, whereby a farmer had a microcomputer (costing in the United Kingdom at present about £2,500) with a set of floppy discs which stored the kind of information necessary to him and the programs to access it. With such a service that farmer would never need to darken the doors of a library again: which is of course to make the unwarranted assumption that he had ever used libraries in the first place. One striking effect of the new technology will be to make information available *for the very first time* to some sectors of the community. There is undoubtedly going to be – in the words of Roger K Summit[8] – 'a new influx of information users who were previously put off by or unable to utilize the traditional tools effectively'.

In the office environment, the use of word processors is being developed on similar lines. Reviewing recent progress, John Whitehead[9] remarks that the new office technology era is very much with us here and now: 'Facts and figures are quoted *ad nauseam* on the high current cost of writing a letter, filing letters, memos, reports and documents, trying to communicate with someone by telephone or other telecommunication means and, most significant of all, the high cost of

27

people undertaking these never-ending tasks. The high level of investment in factories and plants and the ever-increasing fight to improve
productivity by automating the dull, routine jobs are usually quoted
and compared with the extremely low investment in improving and
automating the equally tedious routine jobs in the office environment'. In other words, just as the manufacturing community many
decades ago turned to the machine to augment brawn, in present times
the business and commercial community is turning to the machine to
augment brain and memory. More elegantly and academically expressed,
the socio-economic-historical background to today's situation can be
presented in terms of a structure of three industrial revolutions: 'The
first dealt with machines that extended human muscles; the second
with machines that extended the human nervous system (radio, TV,
phones, films); and the third, the computer-based information revolution producing a post-industrial economy, deals with machines that
extend the human brain'. (Professor Tom Stonier of Bradford University,
quoted in *The guardian* newspaper, 5 February 1981).

Whitehead recounts that word processing machines were introduced
originally to mechanize the typewriting functions in offices, but then
their use as computer terminals to access in-house and external databases, as electronic mail peripherals, and as intelligent terminals, began
to revolutionize office procedures. The term 'word processing' (a
translation of the German 'Textverarbeitung') was first used in the
1960s by IBM to describe that company's range of correcting type-
writers. The first word processors were simple machines which used
paper tape as the storage medium and were employed for repetitive
and standard letters. The major breakthrough came with the introduction of a built-in magnetic tape memory device. Next was introduced
a visual display unit (VDU) so that operators could see what they were
typing, and the capacity of the electronic memory was increased.

Whitehead provides an analysis and description of the principal
elements of a modern machine: keyboard, screen, print unit, storage
systems, and processing logic. The keyboard is alphanumeric, with some
special function keys. Input is by means of keyboarding, but the
future does offer other possibilities — including voice input. The screen
on a word processor, at its simplest and cheapest, is a 'thin window'
displaying just part of one line of text, but at the other end of the
scale can be large enough to display two full pages of text. The print
unit is a letter-quality printer, with a higher output speed than the
conventional typewriter. The word processor's storage system is some

form of internal magnetic memory, supplemented by an external storage facility in the form of (most commonly) a floppy disc (also called a diskette) system. A floppy disc's capacity can range from fifty to twelve hundred pages of text. Larger systems can store up to 150,000 pages. Whitehead notes that the continuing downward trend in digital storage costs will make bulk electronic storage cheaper than paper by the mid-1980s. Finally, there is the processing logic. It is the logic in word processors which provides the various functions such as editing, storing and retrieving text, and which controls all the components of the system. In all systems some of the logic is in the form of hardware, that is to say, electronic circuits. On the more modern systems, however, most of the logic is in the form of software fed into and stored in the internal memory.

Whitehead goes on to explain that using a word processing facility to produce reports and other documents, *de facto* creates the facility to store those reports to provide full text retrieval. The system will search each document for key words or descriptors and either list the details of the relevant reports or display the relevant sections of each of the documents on the screen. Abstracts or indexes of external information can be included in the system, and word processors with a communications mode can be used as computer terminals to access external commercial databases.

Thus, as Whitehead concludes, in the paperless environment of an automated office, employees will be able to search for and retrieve whatever information is available to them from internal and external sources. This may be regarded, in his view, as either good news for librarians and information officers: or 'a very large threat'.

Essentially it comes down to the fact that the new technology represents, to quote Dr John Race of Brunel University, 'a new dynamic intermediary between the reader and the text'. It is what Vannevar Bush was visualizing with his 'Memex', what Lancaster conceptualized for the scientific and technical community, what the ACARD report saw possible for individuals at home, and what Whitehead himself describes in the office context. It is what conventional libraries have never been able to provide.

The pre-emptive technology is available, and its costs are decreasing. At the present time the crucial factor is the amount and types of information available for use in electronic form. For five hundred years mankind's knowledge — our communal brain — has been accumulated and stored in printed form. The next stage is the electronic memory.

29

References

1 Nora, Simon *and* Minc, Alain *The computerization of society: a report to the President of France.* Cambridge, Mass., MIT Press, 1980.

2 Toffler, Alvin *The third wave.* London, Collins, 1980.

3 House of Commons *Fourth report from the Education, Science and Arts Committee, Session 1979-80. Information storage and retrieval in the British library service.* London, 1980.

4 Cabinet Office, Advisory Council for Applied Research and Development *Information technology.* London, HMSO, 1980.

5 Oldman, Christine *and* Wills, Gordon *A re-appraisal of academic librarianship.* Bradford, MCB Publications, 1978.

6 Thompson, James *Library power.* London, Bingley, 1974.

7 Lancaster, F W *Towards paperless information systems.* New York, Academic Press, 1978.

8 Summit, Roger K *Impact of on-line systems. In* Kent, Allen, *and* Galvin, Thomas J, *eds. The on-line revolution in libraries: proceedings of the 1977 Conference in Pittsburgh, Pennsylvania.* New York, Marcel Dekker, 1978.

9 Whitehead, John 'Word processing: an introduction and appraisal' *Journal of documentation*, 36 (4), December 1980.

Chapter 3

THE ELECTRONIC MEMORY

In relation to the amount and range of information stored and recorded (however inadequately) in libraries, the electronic memory must at present still be regarded as rudimentary and embryonic. It does not as yet stretch back twenty years. Its subject coverage is heavily weighted on the scientific and technical side. In content it is still essentially surrogate: that is, it is a secondary source of information rather than a primary one. The reasons for all this lie in its origins.

It is curious to reflect that the development of the pre-emptive technology was initially conceived as no more than a way to facilitate the printing of indexes and abstracts. Since the Second World War abstracting and indexing services have had to cope with an increasing tide of publications, particularly in science and technology. The annual production of articles has been estimated[1] as being of the order of 500,000 (Chemistry), 350,000 (Medicine), 350,000 (Biology), 85,000 (Physics), 85,000 (Engineering) and 25,000 (Psychology) — to give just a handful of examples. This quantity of literature has grown beyond the capacity of most scientists to keep abreast of, even in their specialist fields. An inevitable outcome has been the boom in the publication of secondary abstracting services, to enable scientists to keep track of relevant work and be directed to appropriate source journals without having to scan every publication in full themselves. In their turn the secondary services have found processing this great volume of literature, and printing abstracts and indexes, progressively more complex and costly. The situation led in the late 1950s and early 1960s to the adoption of computer processing and typesetting.

As W M Henry has explained:[2] 'The problem of printing accurately, in the shortest possible time, the lists of references in a collection of abstracts is particularly suitable for a computer solution. The correction and editing process is straightforward when the information is in electronic form; the information is held on the computer and can be verified from a keyboard connected to the computer and modified when necessary. Also, the sorting and re-formatting which is necessary to give the different forms of the abstract collection, such as alphabetical author list, inverted file in alphabetical order of keywords, lists in classification order, and other lists, are much simpler when the information is moved round in electronic form. Furthermore, the magnetic tape holding the information can be delivered to the printer and used to produce the printed output directly. The various type sizes and founts, the layout and the text justification can all be produced by signals inserted by a computer program'.

The needs and economics of conventional publication thus gave, as a by-product, full data on journal references in a machine-readable form, making such data available independently for computer searching. The eventual questions had to be, and now are: why print at all? why not accept the magnetic tape on which all of the information is stored as the final, rather than an interim, product?

F W Lancaster[3] remains in no doubt as to the eventual outcome: 'We are at present in an interim phase in the automation of science communication. This interim phase is one in which machine-readable data bases exist side by side with printed data bases. The computer is used to produce a conventional printed publication which is also distributed conventionally. But this must change. At some date in the near future, there will begin a natural crossover from electronic production of print to electronic publication and dissemination (ie to the paperless mode of operation). The same evolutionary process will apply to the production of primary publications, but the evolution in primary publication will lag some years behind the development in secondary publication. By the year 2000, it seems entirely reasonable to suppose that formal communication in science and technology will be almost exclusively electronic, and that a substantial move to machine-aided informal communication will also have occurred. Such changes seem to be simply a matter of economic necessity'.

To return however to the very beginnings of machine-readable data-bases. The pioneering service was that developed by the National Library of Medicine in the United States. Called MEDLARS (Medical Literature Analysis and Retrieval System), it was designed primarily to produce a major printed index, *Index medicus*. Lancaster, who as was noted in the previous chapter worked on the project, describes MED-LARS as 'the first device used in a large production environment for photocomposition under computer control'. To photocompose *Index*
32

medicus it was first necessary to put the indexing records into machine-readable form. Having done so, not only was it possible to generate printed indexes, but possible also to offer to conduct retrospective computerized searches and to provide a selective dissemination of information (SDI) service. MEDLARS was implemented in 1964. With its introduction, information technology may be said to have begun.

The MEDLARS retrospective searches and SDI service were off-line: that is, the search method used was to construct personal subject profiles in machine-readable form, batch these together, and run them centrally against the MEDLARS database. Records which matched the interests of particular profiles were printed out and posted to the individuals concerned. Batch searching is still frequently used, in particular to provide current awareness services, and since many personal profiles can be matched in a single run costs are low. But as a recent guide[4] to information retrieval systems goes on to point out: 'Batch methods for retrospective searching are not satisfactory, since, as tape stores grow, it becomes time-consuming and uneconomic to do lengthy computer runs except where a number of searches can be run together. Another disadvantage of batch searching is that the searcher cannot modify his inquiry strategy during the run. If the references retrieved are unsatisfactory, then the profile has to be amended off-line and there is consequent delay in such a mode of operation'.

The next stage of development therefore was the conversion of systems from off-line to on-line. Lancaster explains in detail why: 'It is clear that off-line systems for retrospective searching (but not necessarily for SDI) have significant disadvantages. The response time may be unsatisfactory for any but the user involved in a relatively long-term project; the system provides no capability for browsing; in constructing his strategy the searcher is operating 'blind' without being able to develop the strategy in an interactive, heuristic manner; and, finally, the real system user (ie the person with the information need) is unable to conduct his own search but must delegate this responsibility to an information specialist who knows how to interrogate the system. On-line information retrieval systems have none of these disadvantages. In an on-line system the users are in direct communication with the computer and with the data base they wish to interrogate. They communicate by means of a terminal, which may be a simple typewriter terminal or some type of video display with associated keyboard, connected to the computer by means of communication lines. Because these communication lines can be regular telephone lines, the

33

terminal can be far removed physically (eg several thousand miles) from the computer itself. Through time-sharing, an on-line system can support multiple simultaneous users, giving each of these (most of the time) the illusion that he is the sole user of the system. Response in an on-line system is immediate rather than delayed. That is, an on-line system can respond very rapidly to a user command, typically in 5 seconds or less. On-line systems can thus be used for searches in which users need information right away (eg a physician needing information to deal with an immediate clinical problem), whereas off-line systems are really of value only to users to whom response time is relatively unimportant. Moreover, the on-line searcher can interact directly with the data base, developing his strategy as he goes along on a trial-and-error basis (ie heuristically). Searching errors are less serious in an on-line system than they are in an off-line system because they can be identified and corrected quite rapidly. Finally, because terminals can be made widely available, and because languages of interrogation can be kept relatively simple, on-line systems can be used in a nondelegated mode. That is, the scientist, intelligence analyst, or other professional who has need of information can conduct his own search at the terminal if he so desires. This is a significant advantage: one of the major problems of a delegated search system is that the user may not be able to describe clearly, to an information specialist, what it is he is looking for, or the information specialist may misinterpret the request of the user'.

Experiments with on-line retrieval began in the early 1960s, at the Massachusetts Institute of Technology in particular, and the late 1960s saw the development of a number of important systems, including Lockheed's DIALOG. In 1971 the US National Library of Medicine implemented the on-line version of MEDLARS, MEDLINE. Proof of the arguments put forward by Lancaster in favour of on-line as opposed to off-line systems was the fact that the conversion of MEDLARS to MEDLINE increased the use of this database in the United States from 20,000 searches a year to 20,000 searches a month.

Just as MEDLARS/MEDLINE derives ultimately from a publication system designed to produce printed indexes and abstracts, so also is the case with the majority of subsequent machine-readable databases. Aslib's directory of on-line bibliographic databases, compiled by Hall and Brown,[5] now lists nearly 200. Significantly this directory is dedicated 'to all those involved in the creation of the keys to the world's knowledge stores – the abstracting and indexing journals'. In the introduction the two compilers provide a statistical profile of this segment of the electronic memory.

Hall and Brown first define an on-line bibliographic database as a collection of records, usually derived from the machine-readable version of an abstracting or indexing journal, held on-line in a rapid-access computer store. Next they calculate that 'the total on-line repertory' contained in 1981 over 70 million references with about 10 million references being added annually. Allowing for duplication between databases, they estimate that there are some 40 million unique references searchable on-line with a further 6 million unique additions annually.

These figures are indeed impressive, as has been the growth rate over the last fourteen years (from under a quarter of a million references in 1968, to 3 million in 1972, 24 million in 1976, to the number just mentioned for 1981). It is however necessary to stress the derivative, surrogate nature of this segment of the electronic memory: these are records, references to the literature, not the literature itself. Even so, as Hall and Brown remind us, 'When it is remembered that the massive indexing operations of the largest libraries in the world serve as the keys to holdings of only some 10-20 million documentary units, it is clear that the power now available through a simple computer terminal in even the smallest library is such as to stagger the imagination'.

As part of their statistical profile of on-line bibliographic databases Hall and Brown next examine subject coverage. It is very clear from the bar graph they provide that the number of references available in Applied Sciences (34 million) and Pure Sciences (over 22 million) dwarf all others, with Medicine next in sight (just over 10 million), then Agriculture (5 million) and Social Sciences and Education (about 4 million). Philosophy and Psychology (635,000), Religion and Theology (50,000), Linguistics and Languages (300,000), Arts/Recreation/Music (220,000), Literature (300,000) and History/Geography/Biography (380,000) are plainly in a different league. Hall and Brown echo the opening remarks of this chapter on the present embryonic state of the electronic memory: 'While the on-line treasury is now very rich indeed, a note of caution is not, however, out of place. Many subjects (eg art) can be searched very intensively on-line, but there are still many fields where on-line reference coverage is as yet less than complete, or indeed non-existent. It is encouraging to note, however, that the trend of recent years — with impressive arrays of new databases becoming available year by year —augurs well for ever-improved subject coverage'.

Likewise in their statistical profile they confirm the present time-span limitations of the electronic memory (bearing in mind comparison with the time-span of the printed word, which is more than 500 years). They present a graph of the time-span available on-line taking 1980 as 100 per cent coverage. Some 86% cover the last five years, nearly half the databases cover the decade 1970-80, and only in a very few areas do 6% of the databases cover over 20 years of the literature (retrospective data punching having been undertaken). Both the subject, and time-span, coverage of course reflect the origins of on-line bibliographic databases as derivatives of abstracting and indexing services. However, Hall and Brown do remark in relation to the time-span limitation: 'While the time-span available on-line is only some 14 years out of the total database existence of 74 years, the time-fraction available on-line is the *recent* literature. This is generally acknowledged to be the most immediately useful portion of the literature for most end-users'. It was presumably on this ground that Roger K Summit, the Director of Lockheed Information Systems, felt able to claim in December 1979[6] that 'most of the significant knowledge recorded during the 1970s is represented by the databases currently available'.

'The reality of the present database industry', comment Hall and Brown, 'is that the very existence of the present enormous on-line knowledge pool is a staggering intellectual and technical achievement, accomplished in less than 20 years. It has required the combined efforts of thousands of people in fields ranging from computing and programming to surface and satellite communications technology. To this must be added the truly enormous amounts of effort poured into the production of the primary databases, whether on-line or paper-based. The existence of the on-line knowledge pool is a remarkable tribute to the small number of original on-line pioneers, and to the even smaller number of far-seeing financial sponsors'. And they conclude: 'It is arguable that of all the information retrieval methods available only one — on-line retrieval — can closely approach the desirable ideal of putting the enquirer *instantly* in touch with a substantial part of mankind's collective memory'.

The on-line database industry, like conventional publishing, is of course a commercial operation. The marketing of access to on-line databases is by way of on-line suppliers: organizations which acquire databases through licensing agreements, load them on to their own computing facilities, and then charge for searches made. There are three major American on-line suppliers: Lockheed, System Development Corporation, and Bibliographic Retrieval Services. In the United King-

36

dom there are BLAISE (British Library Automated Information Service) and INFOLINE (a consortium of learned society, public sector and commercial publishing interests). In France, QUESTEL (a department of Telesystemes, which in its turn is a subsidiary of France Cable et Radio) provides access to French databases. In Europe generally there is Euronet DIANE.

Lockheed's DIALOG Information Retrieval Service, based in California, is the largest on-line supplier in the world. It was launched in 1969 with a single database, and grew from five databases in 1970 to 30 in 1975. Now it has over 100 databases containing some 40 million records, providing references not only (as DIALOG's promotional booklet specifies in detail) to more than 60,000 journals in more than 40 languages, but also to technical reports, descriptions of current research, dissertations, patents, conference proceedings, books, bibliographies, pamphlets, newspapers and legislative documents. The service is available 22 hours of every working day and in more than 50 countries. UK users access DIALOG via one of the special data communications networks through the Post Office's packet-switching service (packet-switching is a transmission method in which the messages containing the data are segmented into 'packets' of fixed or varying length and sent individually to their destination).

BLAISE, the leading UK on-line supplier, was introduced in April 1977, and is notable in that it combines an on-line information retrieval service (to the databases of the US National Library of Medicine and of the US National Cancer Institute) with a cataloguing service (based on MARC records). MARC will be dealt with more fully later in this chapter. BLAISE operates from computers located at Harlow, Essex, and is available during ordinary office hours Monday to Friday.

BLAISE is one of the host services (as is INFOLINE) available through Euronet DIANE, the first direct information access network in Europe. Euronet has entry points in the nine countries of the European Community, uses the latest packet-switching technologies, and its tariffs are lower than the existing international rate since they are based only on volume and time and do not depend on distance. DIANE (Direct Information Access Network for Europe) is the name under which the European hosts (at present some 23) are grouped, retaining their commercial independence and competing freely for clients. Since the European Community operates on six official languages, a common command language has been devised to enable clients to search different retrieval systems using one language.

37

It will be readily appreciated that because the new technology is of such a pre-emptive nature, and because the size and extent of the electronic memory (even accepting that it is still only embryonic) have as a consequence snowballed in the last dozen or so years, there has grown up an urgent need for specialist guidance. This is why in the United Kingdom the On-line Information Centre[7] was established in March 1979 to promote the effective use of on-line services. The Centre is funded by the British Library and the Department of Industry, and operated by Aslib. It offers information on demand to any UK-based user or potential user of on-line services. During its first year most enquiries were requests for information on specific systems or data-bases, and for lists of databases covering particular subjects. The Centre also acts as the UK Euronet Centre and is actively collecting information on the Euronet DIANE hosts and databases.

The activities of the Centre cater particularly for the newcomer to on-line searching. Expertise in using on-line methods has of course developed as the systems have become more widely available, and indeed the Centre is itself an example of such expertise. Skill in on-line searching is by no means as yet commonplace, certainly not in the United Kingdom. Whereas the number of on-line searches in the United States was expected to reach 2-3 million per annum during 1980,[8] and to continue to increase annually by a quarter of a million, the equivalent search figure for Western Europe in 1980 was only in the region of a half-million, though Euronet DIANE is expected to bring databases to the same level of importance in Europe by the mid-1980s as they cur-rently hold in America.

The principles of on-line searching are simple enough, and are adequately described in the growing number of guides and manuals now available. The introduction to on-line searching published in 1980 by W M Henry, J A Leigh, L A Tedd and P W Williams, provides the following straightforward account.

'Searching is performed by looking for a match between search terms and terms stored in the description of the journal article. These terms may be phrases such as *information retrieval* or *library manage-ment systems*, or words such as *information*, *retrieval*, etc. There are also methods to allow for uncertainty. For example, COMPUT? will give a match with all phrases beginning with these six letters, such as *computer, computing, computable, compute, computation, computer-aided design, computer systems*, etc. Also ON*LINE will match with
38

online, on-line and *on line*. In some systems there are methods to allow for matching a fragment of a word, which is particularly useful for chemical names. These searches may be restricted to terms from an approved thesaurus of controlled-language terms which indexers and searchers must use, or alternatively a free-language system may be used where a searcher can use any words that seem descriptive of the search topic. Matches may be sought with terms from many sections – for example, the title, the abstract, the indexing field – or a search may be made for a particular author name or journal name, or the name of the sponsoring institution of the author. In some subjects there are also standard classification codes which can be used for searches. These possibilities give very flexible search systems, and individual search terms can be combined by specifying either that any of a number of terms must be present or that all of a number of terms must be present. The searching process typically starts with a searcher choosing search terms either by consulting printed dictionaries of approved terms or by inspecting the dictionaries stored in the computer by printing out sections at the terminal. The selected terms are then fed into the computer. At each stage the number of items referenced under a selected search description is printed, so that the user can modify the search by combining terms, or by trying new terms, until a reasonable number of items has been selected from the database. The selected items can then be printed either online at the terminal, when there is a small volume of printed material, or offline at the site of the computer, from where they are despatched by post to the user. The selected items can usually be printed in a variety of ways: in a short format, such as an abstract number; or as abstract number and title; or as full bibliographic reference – that is, author, title, journal reference, classification codes, indexing terms; or as full bibliographic reference plus an abstract of perhaps 600 words.'

It is common practice for on-line searches to be conducted in tandem: that is, with the enquirer (who has the subject knowledge) himself present, and a librarian/information officer (who has experience of on-line systems). As Lockheed's DIALOG own booklet observes, 'a trained librarian is often the best choice for conducting searches'. DIALOG's view is shared by T C J Norton and S A Thornton, two librarians whose work at the Royal Aircraft Establishment at Farnborough, Hampshire, involves considerable and constant use of on-line systems (particularly that of ESA, the European Space Agency). Norton and Thornton consider that the main expertise required is that acquired by any librarian as a result of training in librarianship and actual experience of library work, and cite as of especial importance a librarian's developed skill in interviewing clients to ascertain precisely what information they are seeking. Every librarian can recount stories of astonishingly oblique approaches by users to their information needs: like the reader wanting a book on Italian painters because he believed the name of the man his daughter had run away with was Botticelli. Norton and Thornton also consider that it is easier to teach on-line techniques to a librarian than it is to teach professional librarianship skills to an on-line technician or an individual subject enquirer. They rate librarianship skills higher than subject knowledge in on-line searching.

Indeed the impression gained by any traditionally trained librarian observing an on-line search is that it is quite typical of all reference work: a search can be of mixed success, but in the hands of a competent operator does eventually deliver the goods, and is in the end dependent on the quality of the reference tool (in this case the database) used.

The cost of any information search in any mode is always of importance. On-line searching attracts particular attention because (as the British Library Association's policy statement on charges for on-line services[9] pointed out), with very little administrative work the cost of providing the service is easily determined and just as readily passed on to the user. In contrast the costs of traditional library services are altogether more difficult to calculate on an individual search basis, and involve a time-consuming (and therefore infrequently conducted) computation of payroll plus purchase of stock plus accommodation and services costs.

On-line search costs divide into database charges and telecommunications charges, with further charges for printing out references. The DIALOG booklet quotes for a typical ten-minute search a charge in the range $5-8 to approximately $15. W M Henry's introduction to on-line searching notes that the present range of database charges is somewhere between $20 and $150 per hour[2] with most of the major wide-interest files in the $40-60 range. The telecommunications charges are however the more substantial problem and can, especially in the United Kingdom, be higher than the database charges. Norton and Thornton contrast on-line telecommunications costs of, on average, $5 per hour in the United States with costs ten times that amount in the United Kingdom. They are critical of the British GPO's monopoly in telecommunications, and of its level of efficient response to the on-line
40

revolution (mentioning as an example of the latter the GPO's apparent assumption that on-line searchers possess the keyboard competence of data processing staff). This criticism is all the more significant in the light of a comment made by M W Hill at a seminar (organized by the Standing Conference of National and University Libraries) in January 1981: namely, that there is now more data transmission on telephone lines than voice transmission.

HATRICS (Hampshire Technical Research Industrial Commercial Service) calculated in 1979 that the on-line search charges for the British user (both database and telecommunications costs but excluding staff costs) of DIALOG were £75 per hour, and for BLAISE £40 per hour. As a rule-of-thumb most British users have become accustomed to think in terms of £1 a minute, and of an average search costing in the region of £20-30.

Without contradicting the prediction of Professor Meadows mentioned earlier — that the number of on-line searches in Western Europe will show a large increase by the mid-1980s — the fact must be faced that present telecommunication charges in the United Kingdom constitute an inhibiting factor. It is a wry popular comment at the moment that soon the only way anybody will be able to afford the use of their telephone will be by making calls in the dead of night and even then speaking at a gabble. It would behove the government to do more to facilitate our society's access to the electronic memory, just as in the mid-nineteenth century it helped to facilitate access to libraries, the communal memory of that era.

While there is some concern over the cost of on-line services, there is complete unanimity as to their effectiveness. T C J Norton[10] has cited the main advantages as follows:

— Easy and rapid access to a wide range of databases, many of which may not be available locally. Occasional access can be made to databases which could not be justifiably purchased in printed form (not to mention storage limitations). Information is bought when needed instead of being routinely bought as an insurance against possible need.

— The user is an active participant and can adjust his search strategy and recover from errors of poor query formulation. A whole database can be re-searched if necessary whereas this would be a formidable and boring task with large numbers of printed index volumes.

— Elimination of tedious note-taking, typing and photocopying which is characteristic of manual searching. Output can be sorted in different

41

ways — by author, title or journal and compiled in a form useful for the requester.

— On-line databases can be searched by many more access points than a printed index. For example, a database may have 15-20 index terms assigned to each item and all of these can be searched; the corresponding printed version would be limited to four or five index entry points for cost reasons.

— The database is normally much more up to date than the corresponding printed indexes.

— Closer contact with users. Most searches are done by a librarian/ information officer and it is helpful to have the user present to help direct the search by identifying suitable keywords, changing the search strategy where necessary and suggesting the follow-up of fruitful lines of enquiry which often unexpectedly suggest themselves in such a 'conversational' method of working.

Norton's list is amplified and refined by many other commentators. Hall and Brown preface their international directory of databases by stressing the speed ('a speed which no human can hope to match') of on-line searches. Certainly there is no comparison between a machine search lasting seconds or minutes, and a manual year-by-year search of annual index volumes lasting hours. The other major charactersistic of an on-line search is its exhaustive and comprehensive nature, in contrast to many types of manual search which (in the words of Nigel Macartney) can only be done 'haphazardly and partially . . . at enormous cost in staff time'.[11] Actual evidence has confirmed this for all users: an on-line search almost invariably turns up much material not previously known to the enquirer, no matter how specialized the query. Norton's point about the greatly increased number of access points offered by the on-line approach to literature searching is further refined by Macartney — that it is possible to 'combine terms in such a way that sophisticated topics can be searched for' — and W M Henry — that 'an extensive list of synonyms' can be used simultaneously in an on-line search, whereas a manual search would require each to be followed separately, and tediously.

The part of the electronic memory which is represented by on-line databases will inevitably change both quantitatively and qualitatively. The sheer rate of growth of content has already been noted. On the qualitative side, subject coverage will improve, and formatting — that is, how abstracting and indexing is approached — will be modified and

42

revised as the systems become less and less orientated to printing as a final product.

A recent review[12] of the present situation commented as follows: 'There is a considerable amount of complaint in the information business about the quality of bibliographic databases as they are currently available. In their original conception no consideration was given by the database producers to the real information needs of the end user. The bibliographic databases are large repositories of textual data, some of questionable relevance and reliability. During the course of their search on such databases, end users will be given questionable references as well as highly relevant citations. The real problem is to sort the wheat from the chaff — to determine which are the relevant citations and which can be rejected. Many end users are unable to make this distinction and the sheer flood of references obtained is generating resistance within the user community. To cope with this difficulty, various medical experts in the USA are looking at a new form of database which does not just collect data at random. It is a so-called "knowledge database". It has been pioneered in the medical area and involves the use of a number of authorities to review, sift and select the relevant citations, and include only those with suitable annotations. The Lister Hill Research Centre has been investigating this updated review procedure for the past two years. Whilst it was pioneered in this area, the procedure could have similar applications in the broad field of sciences, particularly the behavioural and some areas of the social sciences. The concept is not totally new as a Brain Information Service in California has been doing something similar for several years. Addison Wesley has also been publishing 'Pathfinders' and the Library of Congress has been producing for many years something called 'Tracer Bullets' which aim at getting to the heart of the particular subject matter. The key feature of such programmes is the selectivity, distillation and filtering of raw information — currently disseminated to a busy audience in a haphazard manner'.

But even regarding the situation as it currently is, what has been already achieved in so short a space of time is proof enough of the force of the pre-emptive technology, and of the potentiality of the electronic memory: to the extent that, as W M Henry records in the very first line of his book, 'it is now possible by means of a simple telephone call to gain access to hundreds of information collections containing a total of tens of millions of document abstracts'.

The electronic memory is being further augmented by the input, in a

43

parallel fashion, of data relating primarily to books. Just as on-line databases derived from the adoption of computer processing and typesetting for the production and printing of abstracting and indexing journals, so on-line catalogues have derived from the adoption in the 1960s of computer technology for the handling of cataloguing data. The pioneer here was the Library of Congress.

The Library of Congress's involvement in cooperative cataloguing — that is, cataloguing for more than just one library — goes back a long way.[13] LC began in 1899 to print catalogue cards for copyrighted books, and in 1901 undertook to do this for all its books and to sell the cards to other libraries, thus becoming in effect a central cataloguing bureau for the United States (and other countries also). Much the same idea lay behind the launching in Britain in 1950 of the services of the *British national bibliography*. The culmination of the concept, for both the United States and Great Britain, came with LC's MARC (MAchine-Readable Cataloguing) project, set up in 1964. MARC supplies cataloguing data centrally for current books, in machine-readable form, which individual libraries can then use to produce their own catalogue entries. Though the data for each book is offered in a very full form, individual libraries are able to select only those elements in the record which they consider relevant to their own cataloguing needs. MARC's coverage is very wide, with an international range of libraries supplying data.

The long-term aim of MARC, from its very inception, was 'the establishment of a national communications network for machine-readable data transmitted from library to library, with LC at the centre of the network',[14] eliminating the need for much localized preparation of such data and facilitating the increased use of computers in libraries. In the event the most common outcome was the use of MARC tapes for the production of conventional catalogue cards, so that MARC is still 'wrongly judged by many librarians as merely a complicated computer manoeuvre to produce LC style printed catalogue cards'.[15]

The most substantial embodiment of this view is represented by OCLC, which at the time of writing is turning out 2.5 million library catalogue cards per week. OCLC (the Ohio College Library Center) was founded in 1967 to develop a cooperative, computerized regional network for its 54 Ohio member college libraries. By 1977 it had expanded its services to embrace over 2,500 academic, public, special and federal libraries throughout the United States and overseas also. In the words of its promotional booklet, its two fundamental objec-

44

tives are 'to increase availability of library resources for users of member libraries, and to reduce the rate of rise of per-unit costs in libraries'. The latter objective is further emphasized as follows: 'Library costs have generally increased at a rate higher than inflation, and traditionally personnel costs have accounted for a substantial part of library operating expenses. Prior to the introduction of the OCLC On-line System, most libraries manually prepared cataloging information for each book or other library material — a time-consuming and labor-intensive task. In some cases, the cost of cataloging a book exceeded its purchase price. It could take months for new material to become available to patrons because of the time required to catalog each item. Moreover, the same function was performed repeatedly as different libraries cataloged copies of the same item. The OCLC shared catalog makes it unnecessary for more than one member library to prepare the original catalog entry for an item. Through the economy of scale thereby achieved, the OCLC system reduces the per-unit cost of cataloging an item. The shared catalog also increases library staff productivity and the availability of library materials by reducing the time and number of people required to catalog materials and prepare catalog records'.

To achieve its objectives OCLC designed a computer network system with provision for subsystems: cataloguing, serials control, interlibrary loan, acquisitions, circulation control and remote catalogue access, and information retrieval and subject access. The first four of these are now operational. It is significant, and symptomatic of the whole OCLC approach, that the lowest priority was given to information retrieval and subject access — the two greatest possibilities offered by the pre-emptive technology. OCLC's four operational subsystems — cataloguing, serials control, interlibrary loan, acquisitions — are all resolutely traditional library operations, with not even a nod of acknowledgment in the direction of the electronic library in the electronic society.

OCLC's cataloguing database is the largest in the world. In February 1980 it contained over 6 million records (having reached its first million in 1974, its second in 1976, its third in 1977, its fourth in 1978 and its fifth in 1979). It is growing at the rate of 25,000 records weekly, of which some 21,000 are contributed by member libraries, and the remainder derived from MARC. In terms of language distribution, 75% is in English, 6% in German, 5% in French, and 5% in Spanish, with all other languages being represented by the remaining 9%. In terms of types of material, the bulk is books (87.6%), with 6.1%

45

serials. The residue is films, sound recordings, maps and manuscripts.

Access to the database is limited to a traditional cataloguer's approach — author, author and title, title only. One whole page of the promotional booklet is devoted to a description of OCLC's card production system, starting with the OCLC user at his terminal striking the PRODUCE key, and proceeding to an account of the all-day and all-night operations of OCLC's battery of card printers, with daunting statistics such as the fact that eight tons of paper are used each week (so much for Lancaster's paperless society, OCLC seems to be saying), and that 3,600 parcels of catalogue cards are prepared and mailed each day.

Though OCLC has established a base in the United Kingdom, by means of an agency agreement with BLCMP, the overall pattern which is emerging in Britain is a rather different one. There has grown up over the past few years a number of cooperatives, or consortia, offering various computer-based services to a group of libraries: BLCMP (formerly the Birmingham Libraries Cooperative Mechanization Project), SWALCAP (the South-West Academic Libraries Co-operative Automation Project), LASER (the London and South Eastern Library Region) and SCOLCAP (the Scottish Libraries Co-operative Automation Project). SWALCAP's 22 member libraries (of which Reading University Library is one) have moved away from using SWALCAP's cataloguing database as a means of manufacturing catalogue cards for manual filing into existing library card catalogues, to the interim adoption of microfiche catalogues produced by computer (COM), with the eventual aim — within five years if possible — of on-line catalogues comprised of short entries with multiple access points (author, title, liberal subject indexing).

H William Axford[16] (in a symposium volume with the self-explanatory title *Requiem for the card catalogue*) has expressed concern as to whether libraries in the United States are shaping up to making rational and cost-effective use of computer technology, if 'the prototype utilities that currently provide automated catalog services' are accurate barometers of management thinking. He detects a strong tendency to view the automated database as a *deus ex machina* for irrationally preserving many of the practices and concepts of the pre-computer age of bibliographic control. He singles out OCLC in a radical and comprehensive critique of the extent to which the aspirations of the MARC project have been obscured:

'Let me illustrate this point by some observations on the Ohio College Library Center, which is the highwater mark in the development

46

of automated cataloging data bases thus far and which until fairly recently virtually monopolized the field. It is also the most conspicuous example of the limitations imposed by attitudes that are irrational but powerful vestiges of the precomputer era of librarianship. OCLC is essentially the creation of its member libraries; it is both a beacon into the future and, to some, the source of an illusion that we have already reached the promised land.

'Because it was the first to demonstrate and dramatize the compatibility of computers and libraries, OCLC has become the showcase of the library world — a modern wonder as seductive and compelling as was the Alexandrian Library, which reflected "the glory that was Greece and the grandeur that was Rome" and stood for two millennia as the archetypical library for scholars and librarians alike. Despite its brief existence, OCLC has already established itself as a rival to the Alexandrian legacy, exhibiting imperialistic ambitions and eliciting loyalties worthy of comparison with those of the Alexandrian Library. Yet in spite of its youth, it has begun to show signs of age. It is an innovator that has not been able to exploit the full potential of its innovations. As a consequence, it is in certain respects both conceptually and technologically obsolete, a fact that is sometimes obscured by the size and evangelistic fervor of its supporting legions — of which it is both creator and captive.

'In the first place, there are no authority files in OCLC's software structure. This means that for thousands of titles in the data base, there are variant entries, causing confusion and needless expense at the local level, and raising serious difficulties for incorporating the files in a national data base. Second, the software does not include data-base maintenance and production packages, which would enable member libraries cheaply to provide multipoint catalog access, or to organize their files in a variety of ways beneficial to users — services not possible with the traditional card catalog.

'Library users are increasingly frustrated by the physical limits to access imposed by the card catalog and by the inadequacy of subject access provided by Library of Congress headings. With the advent of the MARC program and the linking of the computer with micrographics, these problems could be solved through the provision of multiple copies of the catalog, supplemental catalogs organized in nontraditional ways (such as by language or area), and catalogs produced in response to individual SDI profiles. Beyond furnishing sequential history tapes, which can then be sent elsewhere for processing, OCLC cannot provide

47

these services. More important, there seems to be very little pressure from member libraries to move OCLC in these directions. In spite of its potential use in interlibrary loans and its planning for serials check-in, acquisitions, and subject access systems, OCLC remains essentially what it has been in the minds of its member libraries since its inception: a utility designed primarily to produce alphabetized catalog cards customized to local, idiosyncratic cataloging practices.

'This situation is by no means due to any lack of perspicacity on the part of OCLC's creator and executive director. In mapping his strategy for OCLC, he was surely aware of the additional problems he would have to deal with when he went to Columbus with the goal of creating the landmark institution that OCLC has since become. He knew that to insist upon a level of sophistication requiring radical change in potential member libraries would only guarantee that the project would never get off the ground. Consequently he had to design a system in which the computer supplemented rather than replaced traditional systems, providing primarily for the customized production of catalog cards. It is within this context that OCLC can be seen as both an innovator and leader in moving libraries toward automation, and at the same time as a captive of attitudes that inhibit the exploitation of the initial breakthroughs.'

Though libraries in the United Kingdom cannot entirely escape such criticism — and maybe the only reason has been that British libraries were not in general conditioned to dependance on a centralized printed catalogue card service anyway — they are fortunate in that their major 'prototype utility' has been BLAISE. As was mentioned earlier in the present chapter, BLAISE (the British Library Automated Information Service, established in 1977) is notable in that it provides access both to information databases such as MEDLINE as well as to a cataloguing database. Its cataloguing database is the four MARC files: UKMARC, current and retrospective, and LCMARC, current and retrospective. They contain the entire cumulated cataloguing effort of both the *British national bibliography* (BNB) since its foundation in 1950 and the US Library of Congress since the beginning of the MARC project in 1968. The files include works recorded through respective Cataloguing-In-Publication (CIP) schemes where information is obtained in advance of publication and together comprise nearly two million bibliographic records of books and some serials. All are searchable on-line. The subject coverage is comprehensive, including fiction, and it is this broad base

48

coupled with the many access points which makes the database unique. In addition AVMARC contains over 5,000 references to non-book materials currently available for purchase or hire in the UK. The records include information on slides, filmstrips, tape-slides and a variety of other audio-visual materials.

Though MARC (as Professor Brian Vickery has observed) was not designed for information retrieval, UK users by means of BLAISE are able to employ it for that purpose on any topic: whether (to quote the two examples cited by BLAISE's own promotional leaflet) pot-holing or origami. Searching is very straightforward. To find books on, say, grandfather clocks, the database can be interrogated either by means of a standard library classification number (681.113, if the Dewey system is used), or a standard subject heading (Library of Congress uses 'long-case clocks'), or the actual terms GRANDFATHER and CLOCK. Such searches, being founded on records for two million books extending back as much as thirty years, tend to be productive.

It is understandable that the House of Commons Education, Science and Arts Committee in 1979-80 was gratified by the potential of BLAISE, and strongly recommended that catalogue records created by libraries in addition to those presently generated by the British Library be made available on BLAISE: such as those concerned with Slavonic, Latin American and Oriental materials, or those covering particular subject areas (such as architecture) and national listings such as the British Catalogue of Music. The Committee stressed the need for 'the provision of the means for the free exchange of bibliographic data'.

P R Lewis, the Director General of the British Library Bibliographic Services Division, sees the use of a national database not so much in terms of an aid to cataloguers (current cataloguing requiring in his view a database of only, say, one million records), but primarily for information retrieval and (as with OCLC) for interlibrary lending purposes. For him the key issue is the means of access: will the records answer the sort of questions which the majority of users ask? Not just authors and titles, and not just terms which occur in titles, but an intensive apparatus of subject indexing. In his judgment BLAISE, though as a database small in comparison with OCLC, represents the right approach. Lewis is not however dismissive of every feature of traditional cataloguing. He would argue that for every book there should still be provided a full 'main entry': first, to provide the maximum information about a particular book; second, because it puts all the information for the user economically in one place; third, because it is administratively convenient; and fourth, because the fact must be acknowledged that in the Western world the name of a book's author has been a key identifying element for so long. Lewis also doubts whether catalogues will ever be *entirely* on-line, and himself visualizes, certainly in the average academic library, a kind of three-tier system of a card catalogue representing the older stock, a microfiche catalogue for current stock, and an on-line system for the most recent acquisitions. His view is that an entirely on-line system would be too linear an approach. Nevertheless he does feel that cataloguing as such will become less and less important, and that bibliographic records must be seen in terms of enabling people to search comprehensively the information stored in books.

The situation in the United States has somewhat changed since (maybe even because of) the comments of H William Axford quoted earlier. Professor Allen Kent in his Pittsburgh study (referred to in Chapter 1), published in 1979, noted the closing of card catalogues in several libraries, including the Library of Congress. More interesting though than any overdue requiem for the card catalogue is the recently reported[17] fact that DIALOG has announced that from early 1982 LCMARC and REMARC records will be offered on-line. In the first instance, the full MARC database, containing over one million items catalogued by the LC since 1968, will be available. The REMARC file will be added in stages, and ultimately every item catalogued by LC under its book classification system will be offered to the on-line searcher for the first time. Also recently reported[18] has been the award of a grant from the Council on Library Resources to OCLC and the Research Libraries Group for a joint study of the approaches, problems and priorities involved in the issue of on-line patron access to bibliographic databases. Allowing library users to have direct access to terminals that receive on-line bibliographic information from a centralized utility is becoming all of a sudden an increasing concern in many US libraries.

As was inevitable with the advent of the pre-emptive technology the dislodging of traditional catalogues is now well under way. Data relating to books is being added to the electronic memory in increasing quantities. P R Lewis thinks it will be as long as 50 years before a substantial proportion of the world's books will be recorded in machine-readable form: no doubt having in mind the fact that at the moment most of the input is from the Western world, in the English language in particular.

But recent news may make a sizable dent in this prediction. The holdings of the two largest national libraries in the West — the British

Library Reference Division (formerly the British Museum Library) and the Library of Congress — are currently being converted to machine-readable form. In a letter to the author (May 1981) David Clements of the Catalogue Systems Branch of the Department of Printed Books of the British Library kindly provided the following information:

'The catalogue of the Department of Printed Books used at the Reference Division, Bloomsbury forms two principal sequences. Material published since July 1975 (and some works published between 1971 and 1975) are catalogued by Anglo American Cataloguing Rules (AACR) and utilize computer based services (LOCAS) provided by the British Library (Bibliographic Services Division). All material published up to and including 1970 together with most works received between 1971 and 1975 are in the General Catalogue of Printed Books contained in loose-leaf volumes housed in the main Reading Room at Bloomsbury and published in several printed sequences (GK3 and its supplements).

'The Reference Division of the British Library is undertaking a development project aimed at retrospectively converting the printed sequences of the General Catalogue (GK3 and its supplements) into machine-readable form that would enable the introduction of improvements in its method of catalogue maintenance, provide the facilities to issue multiple copies of an up-to-date catalogue at regular intervals via Computer Output Microform, provide an up-to-date shelfmark sequence for housekeeping and stock control purposes and create the possibility of interrogating the files in a computerized system.

'The processing required to get the printed sequences of the catalogue into machine-readable form fall into three sequences:

1 transcribing the data to magnetic tape. This is based on the microfilming of over 200,000 pages from the printed volumes of GK3 and its supplements and the conversion of the data into machine-readable form by optical character recognition techniques.

2 error correction. A small residue of errors would remain after data conversion and an editing process will be required for two principal purposes (a) to eliminate any errors in the data remaining after OCR processes, (b) to ensure that the records taken from the published sequences of the GK are brought up to date with the records in the loose-leaf volumes in the Reading Room.

3 automatic format recognition. As a final stage of the conversion, programs will be required to analyse typographical and certain other

51

information in the data in order to break the records up into meaningful units to which MARC type tags can be applied for subsequent record handling in computer systems.

'The catalogue is estimated to contain some 1,000 million characters in Roman, Greek and Cyrillic and it is intended to retain these alphabets in the retrospectively converted records. Current activities are concentrating on the development of facilities to provide OCR systems of suitable performance standards and the provision of appropriate computer facilities to handle the error correction stages.'

In relation to the Library of Congress, REMARC is the name the Carrollton Press of Arlington, Virginia, has given to the database it is creating of virtually every work ever catalogued by that great library. *American libraries* for April 1980 reported on the project thus: 'Since 1968, the Library of Congress has put more than one million recent bibliographic records into a machine-readable form (MARC), usable in computer-assisted library operations throughout the world. But some 5.2 million records in LC's classified collections, many of them for foreign materials plus items catalogued before 1968, did not get into MARC, and must be put into machine-readable form by each library wanting such access. Now, working at a rate of about 1.4 million a year, Carrollton will put these records into an abbreviated but quite useful MARC format (REMARC) and offer the massive database for distribution — ie, for on-line searching and off-line printout by author, title, subject, series, LC call number, and LC card number'.

The move to on-line databases encompassing the world's books does not end there. As P R Lewis reported to the author, there are also numerous other networks in the United States: ARLIN for example, which has more potential than even OCLC. Among other bibliographic database ventures there is that of the Dawson Publishing company which is creating a catalogue of eighteenth-century British books by amalgamating, in computer files, the relevant holdings in the main catalogues in the British Library, the Bodleian Library and the University Library, Cambridge. The paramount intention has been to provide as many useful cross-references and points of access to data as possible, including a subject approach.

In concluding this survey of the two current major components of the electronic memory — databases derived from abstracting and indexing journals, and databases relating to books — the point must be made again that both components are limited in the sense that they are biblio-

52

graphic databases, surrogate records. They track the source, not the document itself. What are also needed are links between these elements – rather in the way Fremont Rider sought to have a microform version of a book on the back of the card catalogue entry for that book. Otherwise we are left with a large residue of the classic problems of the unusable library, described in the first chapter of this work. What is now required is a data bridge.

References

1 HATRICS *Notes on on-line information retrieval.* Winchester, Hampshire County Library, 1979.

2 Henry, W M *and others. On-line searching: an introduction.* London, Butterworth, 1980.

3 Lancaster, F W *Towards paperless information systems.* New York, Academic Press, 1978.

4 HATRICS, *op.cit.*, 1.

5 Hall, James L *and* Brown, Marjorie J *On-line bibliographic databases: an international directory.* 2nd ed. London, Aslib, 1981.

6 *Outlook on research libraries,* 2(2), February 1980, p14.

7 Johnston, Susan 'Online Information Centre' *State librarian,* 28(2), July 1980.

8 Meadows, Arthur Jack *New technology developments in the communication of research during the 1980s.* Leicester, Primary Communications Research Centre, 1980.

9 Library Association *Policy statement on charges for on-line services.* London, Library Association, *n.d.*

10 Norton, T C J 'Information retrieval' *In* North Atlantic Treaty Organization. Advisory Group for Aerospace Research and Development. *Manual of documentation practices applicable to defence-aerospace scientific and technical information.* Vol III.

11 Macartney, Nigel 'Audio-visual techniques in higher education and research: finding the literature' *British Universities Film Council newsletter,* no. 42, February 1981.

12 *Outlook on research libraries,* 3(7), July 1981, pp3-4.

13 Thompson, James *A history of the principles of librarianship.* London, Clive Bingley, 1977.

14 Quigg, P J *Theory of cataloguing.* London, Clive Bingley, 1966.

15 Tait, James A 'Cataloguing' *In* Whatley, H A *ed. British librarianship and information science, 1966-1970.* London, Library Association 1972.

16 Axford, H William 'The great rush to automated catalogs: will it be management or muddling through?' *In Requiem for the card catalog: management issues in automated cataloguing.* Ed. by Daniel Gore, Joseph Kimbrough and Peter Spyers-Duran. London, Aldwych Press, 1979.

17 *Outlook on research libraries*, 3(6) , June 1981, p11.

18 *Outlook on research libraries*, 2(8), August 1980, p11.

Chapter 4

THE DATA BRIDGE

The entire range of forms the data bridge might take has yet to be established. The most important which have emerged so far include document delivery services, facsimile transmission, full-text systems, electronic publishing, teletext and viewdata (or videotex), and video discs. Two other developments — optical character recognition and machine translation — are also likely to have a significant effect.

It was a foregone conclusion that ready access to the millions of surrogate references in the on-line bibliographic databases would lead to increased demand for access to the documents themselves. Database searching in a sense has done no more than highlight 'the impoverished situation with regard to the provision of full text backup services',[1] though it has perhaps independently exacerbated the situation in that the 'on-line retrieval systems have extended coverage and awareness of more obscure serials'.[2] Professor A J Meadows[3] has attempted to quantify the current level of demand. In the countries of the European Economic Community it is estimated to be around 6 million documents per annum, and growing at half-a-million per annum, with the prospect of reaching a figure of over 14 million by the mid-eighties. It is easy to accept therefore the diagnosis of Roger K Summit, the Director of Lockheed Information Systems, that one of the main problems facing the information industry in the 1980s is the provision of source documents corresponding to retrieval citations.[4]

Initially the problem has been tackled by applying the standard library procedures of loans and photocopies. The United Kingdom is fortunate in having a unique national facility for such procedures, the British Library Lending Division at Boston Spa, Yorkshire. A well-organized central source of supply, notes the British Library's Annual Report for 1978-79, has the intrinsic advantages of first, improving the total national provision of literature, and second, being in a better position to supply requested items more readily and more quickly than any cooperative effort organized by individual libraries (which after all have to look to their own clients' interests first). Hence the proposals, no doubt stimulated by the success of the BLLD model, which were mooted in the United States and in France for a National Periodicals Center and a Centre National de Pret respectively.

BLLD has a stock of 4 million volumes (books and serials), 2.5 million documents in microform, 1,296 miles of roll microfilm, and subscribes to 54,000 current serials, a coverage which enables it to satisfy 80-90% of all loan/photocopy requests made of its service. Annual requests from United Kingdom users run at a level exceeding 2 million. Requests from overseas run at half-a-million per annum, representing some 4,000 users in over 100 countries.

The pre-emptive technology manifested itself in a specific fashion at the BLLD with the setting up, in December 1978, of the BLAISE Automatic Document Request Service, which enables users to check references on-line on the BLAISE files and request them from BLLD automatically. Approaches are in hand from other major database hosts such as INFOLINE, Lockheed, System Development Corporation and the European Space Agency for similar links. As HATRICS (the Hampshire Technical Research Industrial Commercial Service) commented in the year following the introduction of the BLAISE Automatic Document Request Service, the advantages of the system include the elimination of request form filling and of postal delay in sending requests. Altogether more important than these clerical gains is the fact that the system represents a small but important step towards substituting communication for transportation, in one direction at least. The loans/photocopies themselves of course still have to come by van or mail. Use of the BLAISE Automatic Document Request Service is still proportionately small, and one reason must be that many libraries have of course been using communication instead of transportation for several years now in their dealings with BLLD, in the form of Telex.

Lockheed's DIALOG in its turn has initiated DIALORDER, a document delivery service which permits the customers of DIALOG index and abstract databases to use their terminals to order the full text of documents from a choice of some 35 suppliers, including government agencies and commercial document suppliers. The customer simply types in the DIALOG accession number for the document cited and the order is transmitted automatically to the supplier. Nor is the customer limited to documents cited in DIALOG databases: he may order *any* document. There is no additional charge for the service

56

beyond the normal connect time for the database in which the order is placed. The document suppliers invoice the customer directly for the documents ordered, and the customer is advised of their rates in advance. SDC (System Development Corporation) offered a similar service — though the customer had to type in a full citation, not just an accession number — several years before the DIALORDER service, in conjunction with some of the databases available on ORBIT, its proprietary computer retrieval system.

A delivery service embracing books, serials and photocopies has been developed by OCLC. Linked to each of the several millions of machine-readable bibliographic records in OCLC's On-line Union Catalog are location symbols identifying the institutions which have processed the item through OCLC's Cataloguing Subsystem. A library wishing to borrow an item requests a display of symbols of the institutions which have catalogued the item. Holdings information for serials is available through OCLC's Serials Control Subsystem. Through OCLC's Interlibrary Loan Subsystem the library which wishes to borrow an item then specifies up to five potential lending libraries. The system transmits the loan request to one library at a time. If that library does not respond within four days, the system transmits the request to the next of the five potential lenders, and so on until the request is met. As with the BLAISE Automatic Document Request Service and DIALORDER, what the OCLC Interlibrary Loan Subsystem is of course doing is to complete the simple link between an on-line bibliographic reference facility and an on-line loan requesting facility. The same simple link is feasible in any of the automated cataloguing consortia set up in the United Kingdom: SWALCAP, for example, mentioned in the previous chapter, has always planned to make some eventual use of the fact that its computer-held files represent the holdings of twenty or more libraries in a (by and large) limited geographical area. While the interlibrary loan service of the British Library Lending Division remains, for most British libraries, as effective as it presently is in terms of cost, staff-time and speed of delivery, this potential of the SWALCAP and similar consortia is not likely to be exploited: but circumstances in the future are certain to change. One of the findings of Allen Kent's Pittsburgh study (referred to in Chapter 1) which would support such a development within SWALCAP and other consortia is that there is a fair porportion of library holdings which 'reasonably should be shared among several libraries'.

It is worth noting at this point, in a general consideration of the various forms the data bridge might take, that there appears to be a noticeable difference of approach between Europe and North America to the problem of providing the individual researcher with quick and inexpensive access to the full text of potentially relevant documents thrown up by on-line database searches. According to a 1980 review[5] of the situation, the European approach involves the latest advances in telecommunications (for example, facsimile transmission), while the American system still relies on 'conventional mail and labour intensive billing'. The review goes on to quote a prediction that in the United States 'the present moribund state will continue for the next five years', but then, with the growth of full text files in electronic form, with growing cooperation and resource sharing by libraries, and with the anticipated tightening of the Copyright Act, conventional document delivery as a form of bridge will gradually die away, and in the 1990s will survive only in a 'greatly diminished' form.

The European Economic Commission is actively pursuing the use of facsimile transmission (fax) as the basis for a full document delivery service of scientific and technical articles. Copyright however remains a major hurdle, and there are still technical problems. The newest concept in Europe is ARTEMIS, whereby the scientific community would be linked through Euronet by a network of facsimile distribution. Publishers would supply copies of the requested full text to the library (or other user) by overnight fax, at a third of present transmission rates.

It should be added that the 1980 review of the current situation just referred to, which compares the European with the North American approach, is not entirely fair to the latter in that the use of facsimile transmission has also been explored in the United States. As early as 1967, as Barrett and Farbrother[6] record, a pilot programme was conducted by the Division of Library Development of the New York State Library, the FACTS programme ('Pilot project in the facsimile transmission of library materials'). The results of the programme were however very disheartening: the equipment was found to be inadequate, the service slow, and the demand unexpectedly low.

As a technology facsimile transmission is more than a century old. Its main use before the Second World War was for the transmission of photographs for newspapers. The principle on which it operates is that a transmitter scans a photograph or document and converts the images into electrical signals. The electrical signals are sent over telephone lines to a receiver, which reconverts them into images. Barrett and Farbrother remark that technical development has been slow.

58

Webster[7] has identified the main problems as, first, the slow speed of transmission, second, the high telephone line cost, and last, the fact that the machines themselves are expensive. Verina Horsnell, the Bibliographic and Information Systems Officer of the British Library Association, maintains that facsimile transmission is too pricey, that there are considerable copyright problems and that there are not all that many machines around. She also expressed to the present writer the general view that facsimile transmission is as yet only at the development stage, not the implementation stage.

Cawkell,[8] on the other hand, draws attention to the fact that facsimile transmission, though an old technology, has been boosted by the adoption of methods of data compression made possible by compact, reliable and inexpensive electronics. He reports that three groups of machines have been internationally agreed upon: Group 1 (which take 6 minutes to transmit an A4 page of text); Group 2 (3 minutes); and Group 3 (1 minute). Details for a Group 4 (with a yet shorter transmission time) are being discussed. Analogue transmission is used for Groups 1 and 2, and digital transmission with data reduction for Group 3. Data reduction involves coding methods which take into account redundancy in the image (for example, large blank areas in a document). The higher cost of the faster machines is of course balanced by reduced transmission costs.

Webster points out that the higher the degree of resolution required, so the time of transmission is increased. Such is the 'density' of the pages of most library material, as opposed to standard business documents, that the expected 1 minute per page transmission time of Group 3 machines would in practice not be achieved. When the British Library investigated the use of facsimile transmission in 1979-80, the average speed was found to be 3-4 minutes per page, and therefore only some 12 articles per day could be transmitted by a single machine: a level of operation of very little value.

Another part of the problem relates to books, as opposed to documents or pages from articles. For the facsimile transmission of a book it is at present first necessary to make photocopies of the book's pages. Such a clumsy, slow and uneconomic method is plainly unlikely to be a significant long-term element in the data bridge. M P K Barnes, the Librarian of Westminster City Libraries, London, has pointed out to the author that since interlibrary loans in the public library field are primarily in the shape of books, facsimile transmission is not currently for him a relevant technology.

Webster does note however a further possible development: micro-facsimile. This is the facsimile transmission of material stored on micro-form (microfilm or microfiche). There is equipment which will scan microforms digitally, and produce a paper copy or a visual display unit presentation. The system is however an expensive one. Other developments which might increase the potential of facsimile transmission include satellite communication, and the new technology of fibre optics. Satellite communication offers several advantages,[9] being economical, distance insensitive, and providing reliable broadcast quality. Images and documents can be transmitted and received far more efficiently via satellite communication than via telephone lines. Transmission cost is not only independent of distance, but is decreasing with each generation of satellites. Not only might satellite transmission mean quicker deliveries of high resolution documents via facsimile systems, but 'better slow-screen reception when browsing'. Fibre optics offers a way of transmitting information in higher quantities and at faster speeds through the telecommunications network. As a recent report explains: 'Information is carried along telephone lines by electrical impulses. The rate at which pulses can be sent and received on copper wires is called frequency. The information carrying capacity of any wire must increase as the transmission frequency increases. The capacity is often referred to as bandwidth. The use of lasers transmitting light pulses along fibre optic cables is on the verge of revolutionizing the distribution of information. The advantage of glass fibre is that it is only one percent of the weight of copper wire with equivalent bandwidth. Furthermore, glass fibres are safer because they carry light pulses rather than electricity. The cables are expected to be highly resistant to wear and weather, though they will cost much less than conventional copper cables'.[10] Relevant to facsimile transmission is that the new technology of fibre optics would reduce costs considerably, radically enhance the quality of reproduction and improve the speed of transfer.

Even so, at the time of writing, facsimile transmission as an element in the data bridge remains as embryonic as when reviewed in 1979 by Webster, who concluded that the routine use of facsimile for transmitting items such as whole journal articles does not yet appear to be a viable proposition. The best application Webster could suggest was the sending of loan requests (that is, the requests themselves) by facsimile, since they are like the business correspondence for which facsimile transmission was primarily designed. Dr Hugh Pinnock, of the British

Library Research and Development Department, who has been very much involved in investigating the library and information potential of facsimile transmission, is nevertheless convinced that this will be the bridge which will revolutionize interlibrary loans. Likewise, Roger K Summit, Director of Lockheed Information Service, believes that in the long-term 'broadband facsimile transmission systems scheduled for the next few years will eliminate the physical constraints and time delays of postal service delivery'.[11]

Certainly though, it seems unlikely that facsimile transmission will ever be used to any large extent for simple text transfer. This was the conclusion of another report, by Kirstein.[12] Only when 'the source data is in paper form and contains graphical material, or the exact facsimile is significant', does facsimile transmission come into its own.

The pre-emptive technology, and the growing electronic memory, most surely both lodge a requirement that the full text of documents be stored, just as the surrogate references have been stored: electronically, and accessible on-line.

F W Lancaster[13] records that full-text systems have already begun to be employed, particularly in the field of law. The groundwork was laid at the Health Law Center of the University of Pittsburgh, which in about 1960 began to put the statutes of the State of Pennsylvania into machine-readable form and went on to add further substantial bodies of legal text. This was so successful a venture that it was later converted to a commercial enterprise (the Aspen Systems Corporation), and adopted by the Department of Defense as Project LITE (Legal Information Through Electronics).

In the United Kingdom, the famous law publishing firm of Butterworth (as Butterworth Telepublishing Limited) have likewise endorsed the commercial viability of a full-text system by launching LEXIS. LEXIS gives lawyers and accountants access to millions of pages of case law, statutory material and other legal sources, updated weekly. The service began in 1981. Subscribers get a terminal, on which the results of their searches can be either displayed on a VDU or printed on a line-printer. There is a variety of search possibilities: case or statute citations with or without a subject context, for example, or the opinions of particular judges on particular subjects. The promotional booklet offers a photograph which tells it all: in the foreground, a LEXIS terminal on a desk-top, with a few sheets of paper and a pen alongside it: in the background, solid ranks of shelves of the myriad volumes of the All England Law Reports.

61

In Europe as a whole 1981-82 saw the launching of CELEX, an inter-institutional system set up by the Legal Service of the European Communities Commission, to computerize the retrieval of Community law documents. Sharing in its operation will be the Parliament, Council, Court of Justice, Economic and Social Committee and the Court of Auditors. The documentation system will include the Treaties establishing the European Communities (and the Treaties amending or supplementing those Treaties), legal acts resulting from the external relations maintained by the European Communities, preparatory documents and parliamentary records forming part of the legislative process of the Communities, decisions of the Court of Justice, and even questions submitted by Members of the European Parliament to the Council and Commission and the answers to them. The period covered is 1952 to date, with a three-weekly updating. Each document is fed into the system with an analytical part containing over thirty specific headings which may be followed by the full text or a summary, depending on the weight of the document.

Full-text systems are also appearing outside the field of law. It was recently reported[14] that the major American publishing firm of McGraw-Hill is planning to make available the full text of 31 technical and business publications available on a database system. The move will mean that international contributions to McGraw-Hill publications will be sent in digital form from the international source to an editing file, and hence to a tape used as input to the database system. Amongst McGraw-Hill publications are *Business week, Electronics*, and *Aviation week*, along with a number of medical, engineering and energy related journals.

Important to this form of data bridge is the further development of search capabilities. Another recent report[15] describes a new computer software package which would allow the free-text searching of full-length articles. In the case of the on-line bibliographic databases the search by keyword is of course limited to keywords in titles and abstracts. The new software package developed by ICL and known as CAFS-800 (CAFS is the abbreviation for Content Addressable File Store) permits the full text of any article to be searched. At present the drawback to CAFS-800 is its file size: that is, its storage potential is inadequate by present-day journal article standards. However, as the report goes on to note, if the storage potential could be upgraded, the adoption of a free-text indexing system such as CAFS would eliminate the need for vast secondary database publishing operations. Abstracts (as the report goes on to comment) are by their very nature second-best to the original full-text publications, and if the latter could be provided on-line, with some method for free-text searching of the contents, then databases of abstracts would eventually become redundant.

Just as radical, and rigorously logical, is the concept expounded by F W Lancaster in *Towards paperless information systems*. In the preceding few paragraphs what has been described is the piecemeal conversion of some full-texts in conventional form — in law books, for example, in some printed journals — to full-texts in electronic form. Lancaster's argument is that eventually the bulk of *original publication* (certainly in the field of science) will be in electronic form. He feels that the present situation is a transitional, stopgap one, and predicts with confidence the gradual emergence of the electronic journal. This topic will be further treated in the next chapter.

The aspects of the data bridge considered so far relate to making the essential connection between a cited source (identified by searching an on-line database) and an actual text (through the agency of a document delivery service, or by facsimile transmission, or by calling up the full text electronically). The pre-emptive technology also however makes possible the direct provision to an enquirer of actual information, actual data. As well as databases, there are now databanks. The electronic memory encompasses not only surrogate references and abstracts (databases), not only full-texts in fields such as law and science, but also information as information (databanks).

The most obvious popular manifestations of databank component of the electronic memory — direct bridges between the user and the information he seeks, by-passing libraries almost completely — are the newly emerging teletext and viewdata (or videotex) systems. In the light of their relatively recent development it is worth defining the three terms, teletext, viewdata, videotex.

Videotex, according to both Leary[16] and Meadows,[17] is the name now used for any electronic system which displays computer-based information on a television screen.

Teletext has been defined formally by Walch[18] as a one-way (non-interactive) communication system that transmits information via television through regular or cable television broadcast signals. A less formal description has been provided for the man in the street in a leaflet issued in the United Kingdom in 1981 over the signature of the Minister for Information Technology: 'Teletext is a service broadcast by the BBC and ITV which provides all kinds of up-to-the-minute

63

information and entertainment on your television screen. It's just like a televised news magazine updated hourly by a team of sub-editors making available about 1,000 pages of general sports, financial and other news, plus a whole range of entertaining topics — all totally free of charge and in addition to the normal TV service. By a clever technical trick, the BBC and ITV can transmit simple drawings and pages of writing, like a jumbo print newspaper, along with ordinary programmes. These are the Teletext signals. They are carried piggy-back alongside the television programme signals. A Teletext receiver, which looks normal but which has a special circuit inside, can tune in to the piggy-back signals and display them on the screen. To receive the Ceefax pages you just tune into BBC1 or BBC2 and switch the set to Teletext; to receive Oracle you tune in to ITV and do the same (Ceefax is the name adopted by the state television service for its teletext system, and Oracle the name adopted by the commercial network). The extra controls on a Teletext TV receiver are very simple; just a modified remote control hand-set like a calculator. Each of the pages on Teletext has a number, clearly indicated in the index pages. All you have to do is to press the appropriate number on the remote control hand-set, wait for a few seconds, and the text will appear on your screen'.

Viewdata is a two-way (interactive) communication system that links databanks to television by telephone or by cable television lines. With viewdata, Walch explains, 'one may use a hand-held calculator type key-pad and have a wide variety of information appear on a television screen, such as classified ads in the daily newspaper, travel and weather information, encyclopedia articles, and even holdings of the local library. Bills can be paid, bank accounts examined, and theater tickets reserved by this new home information service system'. While such systems have been launched in the United States (for example, Warner Communication's Qube service in Columbus, Ohio), the frontrunners have been in France and England: in England in particular, with Prestel, developed by British Telecom.

Prestel (called Viewdata, originally) was conceived by the British Post Office around about 1970, when a research team, considering how the telephone network might be put to more profitable use outside normal hours, came up with the idea of a community information system. The Post Office would provide the computer and the telephone network, and then sell space to anyone wishing to put information on the system. Andrew and Horsnell[19] note that the intention was to design the system so that the cost to users would be minimal, and that the information providers (IPs) would at least recoup their costs. Instead of a terminal (the expense of which would deter the household user), a specially modified television set was developed; and instead of a keyboard (the normal way to communicate with a computer) a hand-held keypad was designed, whereby the few simple instructions required to interrogate the system could be operated by the user on the basis of the combination of the numbers 0-9 plus two special symbols designated * and #. From the databank end the concept was to offer information in 'pages' (or frames), each page being the equivalent to the amount that would normally fill a television screen. This makes it possible to construct a new page or to update (edit) a copy of an existing page without interfering with the system. When the page is completed it can be inserted in the system in a fraction of a second.

The information providers, Andrew and Horsnell also note, pay both an annual overall fee, and a frame rental charge per frame per year. An information provider in addition requires an editing terminal and has to pay computer access costs whilst inputting. Institutions (libraries, for example) can cooperate to form an umbrella IP, and thus pay only a share of the IP fee and the cost of providing an editing terminal. To the user the costs are the rental of a Prestel receiver; local telephone rates whilst connected to Prestel; time-based charges for use of the computer, payable to British Telecom Prestel, at a rate of 3p per minute in (roughly) office hours or 3p per 3 minutes at other times; and, lastly, a page charge to the IP which is set by the IP and can vary from 0p to 10p or more per page.

Post Office field trials of Prestel started in late 1978 in London, Norwich and Birmingham. The public launch was in 1979, over a million pounds was spent on advertising the service, and British Telecom have so far invested many millions of pounds of capital in establishing it.[20] In September 1981 Gillian Leary[21] reported that Prestel by that time contained 180,000 pages of information (65% of which carried no page charge) of an enormous variety, ranging from business information, to tourist and travel information, weather, government information of all kinds, and even games and recipes. Gillian Leary also reported another development, the 'Gateway' system, whereby the Prestel network 'will be used to put people in touch with external databases via their own Viewdata terminals. Obvious applications are in banking, shopping and travel as well as information retrieval. You may soon be online to your own bank (with suitable security passwords, of course!) from your own home — or able to get through to DIALOG or BLAISE. The advantages of using Prestel rather than dialling direct to the latter systems are the ease of use and ease of payment since only one bill needs to be paid for using all the different systems'. She goes on to stress the essential nature of Prestel as being a medium of mass communication, and to state that 'libraries should be able to play a major role' in its successful development. This latter issue will be more fully discussed in the final chapter of the present work. She concluded by characterizing Prestel as being most useful for obtaining small quantities of fast changing, regularly used information, rather than for large quantities of information which need to be checked systematically. More colourfully, Willis described Prestel as 'a big, electronic reference book' which is 'granny-proof' in its simplicity of use.

Willis also records, however, that at the time of his writing, in 1980, there were only 5,942 Prestel users, of whom 5,215 were classified as 'business' (or institutional). It may be that it will take some time before such a system is absorbed by our society. Meanwhile British Telecom continues its advertising campaign — 'Let Prestel solve your everyday problems' — 'Prestel. The biggest breakthrough in business communication since the telephone and television' — and journalists (Simon Westrop, for example, in the *Reading evening post*, 18 August 1980) confidently predict: 'By the end of the century, viewdata technology and home computers will have been absorbed so completely into our lives that everyone will wonder how we ever managed without it'. It is in the immediacy of the information, as Verina Horsnell pointed out to the present writer, that the strength of Prestel-type systems lies. Who won the last Football Association Cup match, who is the world pea-pushing champion, what is tomorrow's weather forecast, which is the best model of washing-machine, where should we go for our holidays? Meadows,[22] while considering that the British Post Office was over-optimistic in hoping that several million home television sets would be fitted to receive Prestel by the early to mid-1980s, nevertheless believes that Prestel has now reached what should be the beginning of a growth period. He is more sceptical of the suggestion (as embodied in the 'Gateway' concept noted earlier) that Prestel-type systems might be used to access other sources of information (via EURONET, for example), but not dismissive: 'The difficulties in taking this step lie less in the technology than in the way the information is handled. The mode of organization of on-line databases is not necessarily obvious to the uninitiated user — which is one reason

66

why information officers are often employed as intermediaries. Hence if access to these sources is to become more diversified, their organization, and more particularly, their indexing, may require a fundamental rethinking'.

This last remark of Meadows does fit in with the scale of chronology which begins to emerge from a whole range of commentators. 'By the end of the century' is a kind of common denominator, despite the present age being one of accelerated change. Professor Michael Twyman, the Head of the Department of Typography and Graphic Communication at the University of Reading, believes that Prestel and its like are not yet truly consumer services. For one thing, he considers them to be too expensive. He does not think that they will be in general use within ten years, if only because we are constricted by the deficiencies of the present systems, which cannot be replaced by anything very much more sophisticated before around about the year 2050. In his opinion the two outstanding defects of present systems are that they cannot cope with high quality pictorial material, and they cannot cope with things that have to be measured. In particular he notes as a typographer that Prestel is limited to small character sets.

Nevertheless, just as Prestel is being promoted in the United Kingdom, so is Antiope in France, Telidon in Canada, not to mention similar developments elsewhere. The vision is that, in the words of Gabriel Pal:[23] 'Networks of large computer centers linked to the national telecommunications systems in future will offer instant access to virtually unlimited information'. Peter Large,[24] surveying the great variety of computer-run public information networks now emerging around the world, considers that these systems may attain their nirvana in the 1990s, and he defines that nirvana as 'the state in which every home has turned its TV set into a combination of schoolteacher, meter reader, banker, home doctor, accountant, travel agent, mail order house, letter box, voting machine, fire and burglar alarm, consumer guide, instant newspaper, encyclopaedia — and government propaganda machine'.

The greater part of mankind's memory does as yet however reside in five hundred years of printed matter, in libraries. The transition to a new age requires the transfer of this memory, at least in part, to a form communicable by means of the new technology. One problem is storage capacity, and here the most promising recent technological development has been the optical video disc.

The principle involved is that images (and sound) are recorded by means of a laser beam burning small pits in a disc coated with sensitive material. From this master disc, plastic discs are stamped out cheaply. Such discs, placed on a suitable player connected to a television set reproduce pictures and sound at will. The applications for the entertainment industry are obvious enough, but as a report by Alan Horder[25] makes clear, the optical video disc has three main features which make it also potentially very attractive for information storage and retrieval: high information storage capacity, low information storage cost, and rapid random access.

Horder notes that already one system currently available, the Philips MCA Discovision, with its 54,000 tracks (the equivalent of up to 54,000 television 'frames') appears to have a much higher information storage capacity than microfiche or even ultramicrofiche. He is quick to point out though that the amount of *text* which can be legibly displayed on an ordinary television screen is quite limited: a maximum of 1,500 characters on a 625-line screen. Horder makes a comparison here with the 4,000 character capacity of a typed A4 (8¼in x 11¾in) page, and the 10,000 characters possible on the printed page of a journal. There is though, as he then indicates, a solution to this problem of character capacity: the use of a special high-definition 2000-line television monitor instead of the usual 625-line domestic receiver, on which most types of printed material could be legibly displayed. Further, he notes that since information on video discs intended for use as computer stores requires to be recorded not in a video (analogue) format but in the way that is universally used for computer storage and transmission − that is, in a binary coded digital form − a single side of the Discovision disc already mentioned used in this mode would have a storage capacity equivalent to one million 1,250-character pages. Horder concludes his examination of the information storage capacity of optical video discs by reporting (but with a degree of scepticism) the prediction in 1978 of the chief scientist of the Xerox Corporation that by the mid-1980s the entire contents of the 18 million volumes in the Library of Congress could be stored on 100 discs. In this context it is interesting to note that Meadows's[26] predictions of video disc developments by the mid-1980s are merely in the terms that by then 'they should become financially attractive as a storage medium'.

By contrast William Kubitz[27] is quite carried away by the information storage possibilities of video discs. In 1979 he declared: 'Assuming that an average book contains 500 pages, each disk (in current use) can hold 1,000 books. The University of Illinois Library contains 5,622,938 "volumes". Again assuming an average volume of 500 pages, 5623 present-day disks are required. Only 563 would be needed for the 10^{11} bit disks, since each of these would hold 10,000 books. This means that only a 2-meter square area of floorspace is required to store the entire library. On the other hand, if one wished to plan for future expansion and used the 30-meter square area that holds 10^{15} bits, there would be room for another 94,370,000 volumes to be stored before a library addition would be needed! Of course, the volumes would have to be recorded. Once in a readable form, the entire library could be copied onto new disks in a few months, working 8-hour days'.

It must be stressed that the emphasis of most commentators is on potential, rather than on 'actually available products or services'.[28] Maria Savage[29] believes that 'the videodisc may eventually become the electronic equivalent of paper and microfilm'. Kenneth Dowlin[30] describes the video disc's potential for the storage and retrieval of information as 'staggering'; Peter Schipma and David Becker[31] write that this technology 'may well prove to be the ideal complement to computer-based information storage and retrieval systems and contribute significantly to solving the problems of document delivery'. David Hon[32] sees the combination of the microcomputer and the video disc as holding 'the form of most design innovations to come. With intelligent and creative design, the microcomputer/videodisc may be destined to take over many of the provinces of both live instruction and the book'.

Alan Horder, however, in concluding his report, not only refuses to confuse possibility with desirability, but concentrates on contrasting the storage potential of the optical video disc with its nearest conventional rival, the microform. He writes: 'There remain, of course, many unknowns. It is one thing to speak of putting the whole of the 18 million volumes in the Library of Congress on 100 video discs and quite another to be sure that users will be content to consult information stored in this form! We hear enough about the problem of "user resistance to microforms". Are we merely going to exchange this for "user resistance to video discs"? Only time will tell. It could, however, be that the greatly increased ease of access to information provided by computer-assisted retrieval which the video disc facilitates, coupled with the control of image quality possible on an electronic display device but lacking on a microform reader, will provide the user with sufficient "value added" to overcome his or her resistance. We should be well on the way to knowing if this is the case by the mid-1980s . . . It would appear that in the video disc we have a medium that within the next decade will come to pose a real challenge to microforms. This challenge will probably be felt most in applications where remote access to information is required. A number of systems have been developed and others are currently in the course of development which will give remote access to microforms by means of some form of television link. Some of these systems propose to use coaxial cables to transmit information; others public telephone lines. But whatever the form of transmission used all involve the conversion of a human-readable image on a microform into an electrical signal. A video disc system, in which the initial signal from the information store is an electrical one would appear to have advantages in this situation, especially if it eliminates the need for the mechanical transport of the storage medium that characterizes large-scale microform stores'.

Horder picks up one other important point in any discussion of storing mankind's memory electronically, bearing in mind the substantial reality that five hundred years of that memory currently exists in printed form. Though commentators such as Kubitz, quoted earlier, gloss over the problem with a phrase such as 'once in a readable form', the *inputting* of material into the electronic memory does constitute a considerable hurdle. As Horder notes, *new* material can be formatted by key strokes on a variety of types of equipment: word processors in particular. The inputting of *existing* printed material presents however quite different problems. One relevant technology here is OCR (optical character recognition).

Meadows comments that with key-stroking the speed of input is governed by human limitations. OCR is governed only by the speed of the machine (which of course can always be improved, and inevitably improved to a level beyond human capacity). Meadows also notes the possibility of voice input, but considers that this will remain predominantly experimental well into the foreseeable future. A news item in *The guardian* newspaper (23 April 1980) reported rumours of a police computer able to transcribe from the human voice, and a security services computer which could tap a thousand telephone calls at once and provide a full transcript of what it heard. The same report did however quote an expert in the field, Dr Frederick Jelinek of IBM's research laboratories at Yorktown Heights, New York, to the effect that his team had persuaded a computer to transcribe sentences read at a normal speaking pace with 91% accuracy, but the snag was that the IBM computer took 100 minutes to transcribe 30 seconds of speech from a vocabulary restricted to 1,000 words.

70

Returning to OCR, however, it was noted in a previous chapter (3) that the Department of Printed Books of the British Library was converting the printed sequences of its General Catalogue (GK3 and supplements) into machine-readable form using optical character recognition techniques, the method being first to microfilm the pages of the printed volumes. Within 20 years, in the opinion of Professor Michael Twyman of the Department of Typography and Graphic Communication at the University of Reading, it will be possible for 90% of the works of the past (in standard type faces) to be read optically without human interface (though of course some editorial work will be necessary).

Another element of the data bridge which must be tackled relates to the language barrier, the Tower of Babel syndrome. Currently the English language dominates the scientific and technological community, and dominates therefore the content of the electronic memory. To make mankind's electronic memory truly universal there must be a bridge between languages, and the pre-emptive technology carries within itself the potential to provide one. The idea of automated, machine translation was conceived in the years 1956-1964, when the computer industry was looking for new uses for the computer.[33] It was found difficult though to isolate the cultural aspects of language — grammar, syntax, colloquialisms — from the mechanical aspects. Barbara Snell[34] has devoted a whole article to the intractability of the former. Many of the early attempts at machine translation were therefore disheartening failures.

A new spirit seems however to have emerged very recently. In November 1981 Aslib organized a conference on practical experience of machine translation, noting that there are 15 to 20 machine translation systems in use around the world and that 'translation by computer is now a reality'. A particular impetus is coming from the European Commission, since in the EEC all information needs to be produced simultaneously in as many as six different languages. In 1977, for example, some 38% of the 8,200 employees of the EEC were involved in linguistic services. The system now proposed by the European Commission is called Eurotra. America has generated a software system known as Systran. In France there is TITUS, an automated translation system used initially in the field of textiles.

It would be wrong to conclude this examination of the data bridge without some acknowledgment of another reality: that technological possibility is one thing, but that actual universal adoption is totally

71

dependent on political, social and economic factors. A recent evaluation[35] of the situation — 'information sociotechnology' is the name suggested for this new area of study — pointed to a number of contradictions and problems: for example, that the 'negative employment effects' of computer/microchip developments conflict with a current birth rate which requires the creation of more jobs; that commercial competition is resulting in lack of standardization in information hardware and therefore creating numerous problems of compatibility; that the aim of each nation to remain sovereign over its indigenous information resources has raised the concept of transborder data flow, and how it can be restricted; and that many countries are concerned with the individual's right to know, and this puts constraints on the development of computerized databases. 'In general', the article comments, 'there is a feeling that the information technology possibilities are threatening to outstrip the capabilities of the individual to understand and adopt them. Unless due attention is paid to the real needs of the users — simplicity, economy, "user friendliness", etc — much of the new technology could become redundant before its time'.

A further theme has appeared in the general consideration of the effects of any of the new technologies (not just those relating to information). A typical example was a newspaper article by John Hemsley (*Reading evening post*, 15 January 1981) which began: 'Whatever happened to the microchip revolution? On countless TV programmes and in innumerable newspaper articles, we have been told that these tiny electronic miracles are going to change our everyday lives. But in most homes in the country, the only effect has been a rash of flash-in-the-pan video games and battery-consuming pocket calculators'.

What is not understood here, and not notably well understood even by commentators who should know better, is that implementation time-scales are impossible to predict. Each development has been, and will be, gradual. As Verina Horsnell was at pains to point out to the present writer, between that development period and the period of implementation, there is a critical point. On-line information services are in themselves a good illustrative example. They were, in development terms, available in 1965; but it was not until the mid-1970s (and not until the late 1970s in British university libraries) that they were in general use.

In particular there is the delaying factor of the economics, the actual cost of the pre-emptive technology and the data bridge. Something new always means a fresh outlay. One of the persistent concerns in the adoption of on-line technology and systems has been cost. In the 'final evaluation' of the 1977 Pittsburgh conference on the on-line revolution in libraries[36] this emerged as 'the major problem'. Verina Horsnell points to another aspect of cost also: the pre-emptive technology has created a debate for the first time about *charging* for information, the simple reason being that these new services, unlike traditional services, can be costed precisely. On-line systems (as noted in Chapter 3) generate bills automatically. Prestel displays, along with information on a television screen, the charge to the user for that information. Until now the British Library Association has set its face against any form of charging for information, a cornerstone of its ethic having always been that information must be free. An even more difficult problem in relation to information is that of copyright, the legal protection of intellectual, literary and artistic property. The very ease with which the new technology can replicate and disseminate raises many difficulties, few of which have yet been resolved.

Nevertheless, having conceded that not only are technological experts unclear as to the rate of development and implementation of the various elements of the pre-emptive technology, and having conceded in addition that it is uncertain chronologically how long it will take for the pre-emptive technology to be fully absorbed into our working environment, it still remains the case that the nature of this technological revolution *is* pre-emptive and will displace traditional methods and techniques. Mankind's memory, as represented by conventional libraries of printed books and journals, has become unmanageable and to a large extent unusable.

This being the case, and accepting the increasingly obtrusive existence of computers and telecommunications, of on-line databases and databanks, of facsimile transmission and full-text systems, of electronic publishing, of videotex and video disc, there arises an obvious question: what then is the future of the present staple of libraries, the book?

References
    1 *Outlook on research libraries*, 2 (10), October 1980, p7.
    2 *Outlook on research libraries*, 3(7), July 1981, p7.
    3 Meadows, Arthur Jack *New technology developments in the communication of research during the 1980s.* Leicester, Primary Communications Research Centre, University of Leicester, 1980.
    4 *Outlook on research libraries*, 2(2), February 1980, p14.
    5 *Outlook on research libraries*, 2 (10), October 1980, pp8-9.
    6 Barrett, R *and* Farbrother, B J *Fax: a study of principles, practice*

and prospects for facsimile transmission in the UK. November, 1975. (British Library Research and Development Report, 5257).

7 Webster, Wendy *Facsimile: an overview, with particular reference to libraries and information departments.* MSc thesis, 1979. Centre for Information Science, City University, London.

8 Cawkell, Anthony E 'Information technology and communications' *Annual review of information science and technology*, Vo. 15, 1980.

9 *Outlook on research libraries*, 2 (3), March 1980, p7.

10 *Outlook on research libraries*, 2 (6), June 1980, p14.

11 *Outlook on research libraries*, 2 (2) February 1980, p14.

12 Kirstein, Peter T *Facsimile techniques for on-line computer networks.* February, 1979. (British Library Research and Development Report, 5506).

13 Lancaster, F W *Towards paperless information systems.* New York, Academic Press, 1978.

14 *Outlook on research libraries*, 3 (9), September 1981, p4.

15 *Outlook on research libraries*, 2 (8), August 1980, pp10-11.

16 Leary, Gillian 'Vast prospects for Prestel' *Library Association record*, 83 (9), September 1981.

17 Meadows, *op. cit.*, 3.

18 Walch, David B Review of *Videotext*, by Efrem Sigel, *College and research libraries*, 41 (4), July 1980.

19 Andrew, Geoff *and* Horsnell, Verina 'The information source libraries cannot ignore' *Library Association record*, 82 (9), September 1980.

20 Willis, Norman E 'Prestel? Never heard of it' *UC&R newsletter*, November 1980.

21 Leary, *op. cit.*, 16.

22 Meadows, *op. cit.*, 3.

23 Pal, Gabriel 'The approaching information revolution and its possible implications for resource sharing in Canada' *In Sharing resources — sharing costs: proceedings of the Seventh Annual Canadian Conference on Information Science*, Banff, Alberta, 1979.

24 Large, Peter 'Countdown on computer data' *The guardian*, 6 January 1981.

25 Horder, Alan *Video discs — their application to information storage and retrieval.* NRCd Publication No. 12. Hatfield, Herts., National Reprographic Centre for Documentation, Hatfield Polytechnic, June 1979.

26 Meadows, *op. cit.*, 3.

27 Kubitz, William 'Computer technology: a forecast for the future' *In Proceedings of the 1979 Clinic on Library Applications of Data Processing.* University of Illinois at Urbana-Champaign, 1980.

28 Saffady, William *and* Garoogian, Rhoda 'Micrographics, reprography, and graphic communications in 1980' *Library resources and technical services.* 25 (3), July/September 1981.

29 Savage, Maria 'Beyond film: a look at the information storage potential of videodiscs' *Bulletin of the American Society for Information Science*, 7, October 1980.

30 Dowlin, Kenneth E 'The electronic eclectic library' *Library journal*, 105, November 1980.

31 Schipma, Peter B *and* Becker, David S 'Text storage and display via videodisk' *Proceedings of the American Society for Information Science*, 17, 1980.

32 Hon, David 'The videodisc, microcomputer, and the satellite' *Training and development journal*, 34, December 1980.

33 *Outlook on research libraries*, 2 (11), November 1980, p7.

34 Snell, Barbara 'Electronic Translation?' *Aslib proceedings*, 32 (4), April 1980.

35 *Outlook on research libraries*, 2 (10), October 1980, pp9-11.

36 Kent, Allen *and* Galvin, Thomas J *eds. The on-line revolution in libraries: proceedings of the 1977 Conference in Pittsburgh, Pennsylvania.* New York, Marcel Dekker, 1978.

Chapter 5

THE FUTURE OF THE BOOK

The age of printing is over. Printing as such is no longer employed in book production. It has been rendered obsolete by the combination of offset-litho, filmsetting and computerization.[1] Gone are the tons and tons of printing type. A huge change has taken place unnoticed by the mass of the public, except perhaps for the fact that there has been an obvious decrease in the typographical quality of books published in the last two decades. Most of the printer's skills developed over five hundred years have virtually disappeared. Reflecting on this state of affairs in a recent radio broadcast A R Turnbull, of the Edinburgh University Press, commented: 'While you were watching television, the book died'.

Letterpress printing will linger on, in Ruari McLean's opinion, in small businesses for many years, because of nostalgia, and because of the costs involved in changing. In common use however letterpress has been completely superseded. 'After five hundred years as the sole basis of printing technology', observes Joseph Raben,[2] 'metal type is joining the spinning wheel, the water wheel, the cotton gin, the steam engine, and now the propeller-driven airplane as exemplars of mechanisms that were vast improvements over those they replaced but that still had to yield to even superior ones'.

Raben notes the irony that while printing constituted the earliest assembly-line production of identical units for cheap mass distribution and is generally considered to have been the first modern technology, it has only in the last few years managed to catch up with automation in other industries. What has happened however is not that an established technology has been improved, but that a radically new one is being developed.

Even more significantly the movement to computer-based editing and composition will lead to substantial alterations in the fundamental nature of the publishing industry, a change of emphasis from libraries to databases, and a revised conception of the means by which authors and readers communicate with each other.

Metal type has been replaced by photocomposition: the process of transmitting light through film on to a photosensitive surface. The key technology though, Raben stresses, is the computer, which controls the timing and positioning of the thousands of light flashes per minute necessary to maintain a satisfactory rate of operation. For the employment of this technology the materials to be printed must be made machine-readable, the information translated from visible record on paper into invisible electronic storage. If all relevant details are supplied — type face, size, position on the page — the original can be reconstructed at any time. 'Our generation', writes Raben, 'still conditioned to visualize information as pages of typescript or print, will experience difficulty in grasping the notion of information residing on a tape or more exotic computer storage devices. Having lived with printed pages, having learned to love the look, the feel, even the smell of good books, humanists may not readily accept the truth that the essence of a book, its soul, can exist as bits of binary information on a reel of magnetic tape. In a neo-Berkeleyan spirit, they often cannot acknowledge the existence of what they cannot see'.

It has become crucial to accept that in this present age paper is only a temporary and partial realization, and that the integral form is the electronic medium. Individual representations made from time to time do not disturb the permanent storage which, perpetually casting off replicas of itself, remains undiminished and unaltered.

Not only, adds Raben, is all machine-readable information perpetually available, but the physical space required to store it is miniscule. Moreover the chief value of this new technology for retaining and reproducing information is that it has no single destiny. The modes of creating tangible copies, already numerous, are increasing. The conventional printed page is only one of those modes.

Raben then asks what he himself describes as the inevitable question: 'If so much can be accomplished without paper, why must it be employed in the final step? If the author can compose on a terminal, the editor edit, the referees referee, why must the ultimate user hold in his hand a bound book or journal? Why cannot this reader, too, turn on a terminal and receive what he wants when he wants it? Why must he receive an entire journal in order to obtain a single article? Why purchase an entire book in order to read one chapter or essay? Shouldn't he be able to scan a list of abstracts (on his terminal, of course), and then call up for immediate inspection the works which seem most apposite to his interests at the moment?'

His answer is that for the moment at any rate, individual choice can operate, since 'we stand at the equilibrium point between two eras'. Lee G Burchinal[3] however stresses the inescapable outcome, 'the inevitable scenario'. Computers have and will continue to revolutionize the transfer and use of information. He sees a parallel between the development of present on-line searching from the application back in the 1960s of computerized typesetting to abstracting/indexing publications, and the eventual effect of current computer applications on primary publishing. 'Beginning with automation of typesetting, computer applications have moved back to on-line editing and make-up, management of subscription fulfillment, mailing, and other business and editorial functions. Computer-readable tapes are now a realistic byproduct from journal publishers. Soon we can expect to see machine-to-machine transfer of article surrogate information from journal publishers to abstracting/indexing services. In the not-too-distant future, the full text of articles will be available from remote sources through a variety of technologies — paper and micrographic facsimile, slow-scan TV, and video disc as well as by computer networks.'

It should be pointed out however that as yet on-line searching has not displaced conventional printed abstracting and indexing publications. What A J Meadows[4] calls the 'crossover point' (though close at hand) has still to be reached.

Meadows indeed notes that, on most quantitative assessments, the printed word is undergoing a boom. World book production figures have been rising at an average rate of 3-4% per annum over the past two decades. Likewise journal titles have consistently expanded in number during the past twenty years. The worm in the apple though is that while all of this has been happening costs are escalating. Labour-intensive activities in the printing and publishing industries have shown particularly steep increases. Book and journal prices have risen at a faster rate than the market can readily absorb. Unfortunately also, higher prices have not been accompanied by any noticeable increase in efficiency in the international distribution of books and journals.

The contrast lies in the corresponding trends for the electronic transfer of information. Though admittedly starting from a smaller initial base, electronic information transfer has expanded much more rapidly in recent years. Meadows reports that the growth of data traffic via computer terminals in Europe approached 20% per annum during

78

the latter part of the seventies. The rate of increase was even greater in the United States. He gives two reasons for this growth: first, the rapidly increasing utility and convenience of computerized data handling, and second, the rapidly decreasing cost, both per use and in terms of capital and running costs for a given capacity.

It is in the context of this contrast between the current situation as regards the traditional book and journal, and as regards the electronic transfer of information, that he talks of a 'crossover point'. He stresses the point however that, inevitably, the situation is not a simple one: 'The question to be asked is not the global query — Will electronic media replace the printed word? — but rather, in any given context — What is the likely future balance of advantages between new media, traditional print-on-paper, and some mix of the two? Hence an assessment of new technology and its impact needs to be done case by case, or, at least, category by category'.

What Meadows does not dwell on is the fact that there have already been too many facile dismissals of the future of 'the book': as though paperback novels, monographs on specialized subjects, encyclopaedias, telephone directories and children's picture books could all be lumped together, and equally together be replaced overnight by electronic systems. Conversely there have been almost as many Luddite defences of 'the book' of an equally unlikely blanket kind.

Meadows's own attempt at categorization is to divide all information into three types: entertainment, reference and educational. He argues, for example, that television may be regarded as 'a growth in information transfer predominantly relating to entertainment', with teletext likely to provide an acceptable 'add-on' capability. For some social groups, he says, the growth of television use may have been at the expense of time devoted to reading the printed word; and certainly, the financial problems of newspapers and some weekly magazines have occasionally been attributed to the provision of news and discussion programmes on television. On the other hand, Meadows argues, bestseller lists now always contain titles which tie in with television programmes, thus demonstrating that television and the printed word can be complementary. Even more sturdily he declares: 'Reading continuous text from a television screen is distinctly unsatisfactory, so novels, for example, will continue to be most easily read in traditional book form'.

Meadows here is however falling foul of the classic chicken-and-egg argument. He is wrong in respect of new novels since it is now a fact that the market and the reading public for the first-time novelist has

79

virtually disappeared; and he is wrong in a more basic sense in that the talented writer of our times is bound to choose to write where the market for his writing exists: television, radio, the stage, or the cinema. Shakespeare after all wrote for the stage and Dickens wrote novels in weekly or monthly parts, both conforming to the commercial and social realities of their era. Meadows's argument does not even hold for the works of the novelists of the past. *Gone with the wind* is familiar to millions who have never heard of, let alone read, Margaret Mitchell. Likewise Galsworthy and Trollope, not to mention Dickens, have reached a vast public through the new media, out of all proportion and quite unrelated to their readership in printed form.

Turning to reference information, Meadows comments on the transfer of secondary services from the printed abstract journal to the on-line computer file, and observes: 'The rapid expansion in the amount of published research over recent decades has made the handling and retrieval of information from printed sources increasingly time-consuming. In consequence, computer handling and storage has become increasingly attractive. The demand for a transition from one to the other is by no means unequivocal. Whether or not computer handling is currently regarded as preferable may depend, for example, on the way in which computer charges and overheads are allocated by the account-ing system of an organization. Computer retrieval may be only margin-ally worthwhile in a university environment, say, whilst fully viable in industry. The result is that secondary services are in a transition period, when both print-on-paper and computer access have to be provided. The problem is that dual production may make both channels financially vulnerable during this transition'. He sees a similar conflict — whether potential customers will prefer to retrieve information via their tele-vision screen or via the printed page, over the next few years — in relation to viewdata systems at home. Though Meadows does not say so, while on present evidence the future of viewdata is still to be resolved, there is every sign, as noted earlier, that on-line searching will eventually replace printed abstract/indexing services: it is the printed forms which have become financially vulnerable.

In respect of educational information, Meadows believes that a multi-media package could quite conceivably replace the book: 'One poss-ibility would be the development of the video disc for this purpose. As with reading for entertainment, however, it is dubious whether lengthy stretches of continuous prose will appear as anything but print-on-paper in the near future. An historical circumstance — the publishing

80

industry's unhappy experiences with programmed learning in the 1960s — may also dampen enthusiasm for experimentation in this area. More immediately, the considerable capital tied up in textbooks will tend to slow down any change. So textbooks may provide an excellent example of a print-on-paper product that is likely to resist rapid modification'. He adds though that specialized research publications are another matter. Despite newly available cheaper methods of production (involving, for example, camera-ready copy), small research communities are experiencing increasing difficulty in publishing their work. Hence the attraction of electronic journals for the transmission of short texts. For longer texts there is the possibility of establishing a system of on-demand publishing. Again, though, Meadows sees the future development of both these possibilities as an open question (unlike F W Lancaster, quoted in the previous chapter, who sees them as inevitable).

In discussions with the present writer, Dr Hugh Pinnock of the British Library's Research and Development Department emphasized that *data* is where the immediate change will be, not *literature*. He pointed out that there is a ready market for certain types of information, primarily technical and commercial information. In his view a system could be developed within the next couple of years whereby, for example (and as quoted in Chapter 2), an individual farmer could have a microcomputer and a set of floppy discs which stored the kind of agricultural information he needed and the programmes for him to access it. Dr Pinnock thinks that such a service would probably be on a subscription basis, organized by a commercial agency.

In Dr Pinnock's view also, all indexing and abstracting services should now be offered in machine-readable form, rather than printed form, as much for human reasons (more effective, less time-consuming) as for reasons of cost. Likewise he thinks that encyclopaedias have become very appropriate for transfer to the electronic mode, if only because the amount of information in the entries is not massive (unlike, say, monographic works). Looking further ahead — maybe in fifteen or twenty years' time — Dr Pinnock predicts that it will then be possible to obtain all the novels of (say) Zola on one video disc.

Mr P R Lewis, the Director General of the British Library Bibliographic Services Division, has drawn the attention of the present writer to another category of printed work which will be superseded: the 'guide to reference material' of the Walford-type, until now an essential tool for all librarians, listing with annotations the major and standard reference books in every subject. In Lewis's own words,

81

'Walford is finished: librarianship of the database is coming'.

Professor Michael Twyman of the University of Reading's Department of Typography has nominated three further categories: telephone directories, learned dictionaries (as long as they can be kept within 96-character sets), and standard reference editions of major, prolific writers (such as the Cook and Wedderburn edition of Ruskin). Telephone directories and learned dictionaries are fairly obvious candidates. Editions of major authors may seem less so, but there are two straightforward reasons. One is that such editions are no longer commercially viable in printed form. The other is that with the development of optical character recognition techniques (as noted in Chapter 4) no expensive human interface is required in the transfer from pages printed in a standard type face, to the electronic mode, except for some editorial work.

Professor Twyman's overall assessment of the current transitional situation is that printing is at present geared to high-level systems (in terms of character sets, for example), and that therefore some modification is necessary for the machine-readable mode. This of course in part was the burden of A R Turnbull's lament, with which the present chapter began, and which without doubt echoes similar laments when Hepplewhite and Chippendale chairs were replaced by mass-produced furniture, or indeed when illuminated manuscripts were replaced by the crudities of early printed books.

In the preceding chapter reference was made to the potential of the video disc, and some commentators — David Hon was one quoted — have seen that potential in specific competition with the book. Yuri Gates[5] acknowledges the possibility of such competition, but only to a limited extent: 'Video disc technology has advanced to the stage where practicable systems are being put on the market. Video discs will probably be sold at prices at or below those of equivalent types of books and they will compete with certain types of books, especially where colour and illustrations are important. It may soon become possible to put whole libraries on video discs of the mass storage type, but it seems more likely that this type of application will be mainly archival, and will not compete with primary publishing of books and other printed matter'.

Gates's statement about the future of primary publishing is altogether too sweeping and too confident. Meadows[6] has written that by the end of the 1980s the overall result of the emergence of the new technology should be an enhanced awareness among the general public of available information transfer techniques. He then adds: 'A question of considerable interest will be the response of the printing and publishing industries to this awareness. Will these industries, based on the printed word, diversify to become multimedia enterprises, or will the new needs be satisfied by the growth of a new industry?'

Meadows's own predictions are as follows: 'Existing publishers will obviously continue to be mainly preoccupied with traditional forms of publication during the 1980s. The big change will be in-house, with a rapid growth in the electronic processing of material. Some larger publishers will move into the expanding field of databases and databanks. New entrepreneurial openings will certainly appear. For example, we can expect to see a growing number of "information packagers", organizing both formal and informal communications on a consultancy basis. Multi-media development will be easier and earlier in the USA than in the UK. Hence, publishers may have to look out for increasing American competition during the 1980s'.[7]

The likely future of the publishing industry was also one of the issues which engaged the interest of the ACARD report on information technology:[8] 'Printing and publishing companies will not in future be using Information Technology only in their traditional activities, but will move into the new fields of electronic printing and publishing, becoming providers of information for Prestel and other viewdata services. The market for some publications, particularly reference books with short-lived information (eg stock market information, holiday booking guides, telephone directories, railway timetables) will be most affected by Information Technology, while books and publications of a more permanent character will be less affected. We do not accept a forecast of the disappearance of the printed book by the end of the century'.

Neither Meadows nor ACARD (the Advisory Council for Applied Research and Development) seem to be aware however that the involvement of the publishing industry with the pre-emptive technology is not principally a matter of whether publishers will or will not continue to publish books, or whether or not they will diversify into electronic modes, but that the whole structure of the traditional chain of information — author, to publisher, to bookseller, to librarian, to user — might not be able to survive in the new age. This was the main anxiety aired by Robert Campbell of Blackwell Scientific Publications in the paper he gave at the 12th general assembly of the International Group of Scientific, Technical and Medical Publishers in Frankfurt in October

83

1980 (and reproduced in *The bookseller* for 6 December 1980).

'Traditionally', Campbell declared, 'the librarian was the publishers' customer but now technology has allowed the librarian and the publisher to be potential competitors'. Campbell then went on to observe: 'The librarian can no longer store, let alone purchase, all the publishers' products and with the development of computerized databases and sophisticated on-line bibliographic services the librarian no longer has the need to buy the publishers' product. Indeed, the ambitious librarian, the empire builder, might dream of a huge worldwide complex of linked national libraries; each national library could conceivably just need to buy one copy of a local publication and rely on libraries abroad for the rest. From then on the computer and the photocopier take over. A library in Australia, for example, no longer has to buy a book or journal published in Britain; by searching on-line the Australian user can locate exactly the text required; a press of the button and the order goes across the world, the British national collection receives the order, photocopies the appropriate text and mails it to the user. The development of document digitalization and teletransmission could allow the British centre to transmit the article in digital form to be printed out in the user's library'.

He notes that the stated aim of the British Library Lending Division at Boston Spa is 'supply via the library as opposed to the publisher', and retails that Library's impressive statistics in relation to its document delivery service. With such a service, he asks, who needs to buy the original journal? Moreover he reports that the Boston Spa set-up is ready and waiting for the further demand for photocopies coming through the Euronet/Diane on-line communication network.

The remedy he suggests (from the publishers' point of view) is that publishers themselves must develop their own document delivery services based on their databases with on-line access: 'The potential is enormous for as publishers move to computerized typesetting they will be able to feed a record of the text into a central database as soon as the text is corrected on the typesetting computer. Users will be able to call up "papers" before hardcopy publication. And it is unlikely that secondary databases which are now dominating the on-line field will be able to compete as they will have to finance tapping the text into their systems. If we can organize ourselves in time it is possible that the higher royalties from on-line systems and document delivery services will actually enable us to reduce hard copy prices in real terms. This can only come about if all users, whether of the original edition, a photo-
84

copy, a videotape or a teletransmitted facsimile *pay their share.* This should be the aim over the next decade. It is crucial to our survival'.

On the basis of the rigorous logic of his main scenario, Campbell's reference to reducing 'hard copy prices' sounds suspiciously like a sop to the more traditionalist of his peers. The logic of the system he describes leaves very little need for any hard copy editions at all. Plainly libraries — where the hard copy market lies — will not need them.

Nor does it come as any surprise, following Campbell's remarks, to read a report[9] that under the leadership of Gordon Graham, the Chairman of the publishing firm of Butterworth, and Clive Bradley, the Chief Executive of the UK Publishers Association, funds have been raised to instigate two major document delivery feasibility studies based on the database (with on-line access) of a group of British academic publishers. In similar vein was a report[10] that in Europe 'a major new initiative has been launched by a group of leading commercial publishers. During the past two years Elsevier Science Publishers, based in Amsterdam, have been investigating the dimensions of the photocopying problem by means of an analysis of the number of requests for copies submitted to the British Library Lending Division. Elsevier were able to quantify the concentration of document demand in terms of titles and publishers. This stimulated a search for a technology which would prove competitive to the existing manual fulfilment of document requests, as it was believed that the adoption of highly advanced computer-based technology would enable electronic document delivery to be made in future by publishers, at a cheaper cost than libraries are able to perform it at present. A laser encoded digital video disc, code-named Megadoc, and yet to be unveiled by Philips, has been adopted. It is potentially possible to store up to 500,000 pages of A4 textual material on one side of a Megadoc digital video disc. However, this storage can be reduced by a factor of up to ten if high quality illustrations are stored as well as text. This latter was considered an important requirement for a document delivery service, and a high resolution scanner and printer is to be linked to the Megadoc to facilitate input on to the discs and high speed retrieval and printout from them on demand. Elsevier has found three other partners willing to cooperate in this new venture. Pergamon Press and Blackwell Scientific Publishers (both in the UK) and Springer-Verlag (Germany) are together funding the further experimentation in the costly technical system. In addition, the British Library Lending Division, which is looking at future ways of performing its lending activities, is participating in the study. If all goes

85

well, the intention is to launch the ADONIS project (Article Delivery over Network Information Systems) in early 1984'. It is claimed that 'research libraries will benefit from the new scheme by gaining more rapid and cheaper access to the required documents. Scientific and technical publishers associated with the database will benefit by being able, for the first time, to receive a royalty payment for each time their particular publications are requested from the ADONIS facility. The royalty payments should be absorbed into the cost savings effected by the adoption of advanced technology in this particular document delivery system'.

It has also been recently reported[11] that the Pergamon International Information Corporation (a Washington-based subsidiary of the Pergamon Press group) has launched VIDEO PATSEARCH, which combines 'on-line database searching of the US Patents file (PATSEARCH) on the Bibliographic Retrieval Service (BRS), with the provision of all related diagrams, illustrations and graphics on a separate video disc system. The front page of an application for a US patent provides space for a summarized bibliographic description and classification of each new invention, together with an illustration of the essential features of the intended patented product. The bibliographic information, including abstracts, for the 700,000 US patents made between 1971 and 1980 has already been loaded on to BRS. In addition, the associated 700,000 illustrations have been etched on to a pack of eight video discs. Pergamon are offering a service to patent searchers whereby, for an annual cost of $6,000, the searcher will be provided with a terminal for searching PATSEARCH on BRS, a video disc player, the set of eight video discs and the software which will enable the user to alternate between the on-line database and the relevant video disc frame by the switch of a key on the terminal. The option of a video printout of the illustration is also being offered. This merger of technologies − the video disc and the interactive search of an on-line bibliographic database − constitutes a significant advance in the dissemination of scientific and technical information. Its potential ramifications extend far beyond the patent field, and Pergamon is reported to be actively looking at other areas where the need for instantaneous backup of illustrative material is necessary to complete an on-line bibliographic search. It is intended that VIDEO PATSEARCH will be available in the USA in late summer 1981, and in Europe by the end of the year with the PATSEARCH database being made available on Pergamon-InfoLine'.

Also on the publishing horizon is the electronic journal. Charles M

Goldstein[12] notes that the estimate for the transition of scientific journals to full electronic printing, including graphics, is 10-15 years (though at the same time pointing out that in the video disc there exists presently the technology for storing journal copy in high resolution compressed facsimile format to support on-line browsing or computer-driven demand publication). Professor Senders has experimented in the United States with the concept of the electronic journal, but the experiment was not a success because in Senders's own opinion 'the man/machine interface is still wrong'.[13] Undeterred by this failure the British Library's Research and Development Department announced in September 1980 awards to Birmingham University and Loughborough University in order to make possible a programme of research into communication between people through electronic networks. BLRDD has described the project in the following terms: 'Electronic forms of communication enable people to exchange information, views and ideas by means other than paper and the spoken word. The material is entered into a computer store by a variety of means, and is accessed on-line through local terminals. Such networks are new and in the UK little explored from the users' standpoint. The problems and costs of using them for different purposes are not well understood. Research is needed to establish what they can achieve at present — or in future, given expected developments in technology; what they cost, and are likely to cost in say five years time; and what problems are encountered in use and how far they can be overcome. Particular attention has to be given to psychological aspects of these problems, since in the end the acceptability of a system to users largely determines the extent of its use. Research should indicate the ways in which systems might develop in future if they are to meet users' requirements. In the first project Professor B Shackel, Department of Human Sciences, Loughborough University, will investigate some of the problems concerned with setting up and using an electronic journal. Such a journal is one in which the normal procedures — writing, refereeing, editing and publication — are carried out by computers. With the help of suitable software an author can enter a text into the system, and the editor, the referees and ultimately the users, as well as himself, can have access to the text at their computer terminals. The subject of the journal will be "computer human factors", ie the science and technology of people interacting with computers. Contributors will be drawn from UK research establishments which have an active interest in this subject from either a computing or a human-science viewpoint. Each will contribute at least one

87

research article and one shorter note in each year during the life of the project, entering the articles on-line to the computer at Birmingham or using other methods including an OCR reader at Birmingham and a word processor at Loughborough. The research team will try to assess the value of these different forms of input, including their relative costs and ease of use. They will also investigate the total costs of a journal and will assess how far users feel that an electronic journal satisfies their needs as a form of communication. Initially the experimental journal will be confined to individual, refereed papers, arising from research. But in order to exploit fully the possibilities of the new medium, the research team will investigate other forms of journal material, such as newsletters, annotated abstracts and workshop conferences, and also other aspects of journal preparation, for example co-operative authorship and interaction between authors, editors and referees'.[14]

The primary publishing division of the American Chemical Society in Washington has also for some time been experimenting with ways of putting the full-text of one of their primary journals on-line. In contrast with the Senders experience, the experiment met with such a positive response that in 1980 it was reported that the Society intended to extend the base of this project: 'The American Chemical Society (ACS) publishes 16 primary research journals; it is independent of the CAS division (Chemical Abstracts Service, producers of the leading on-line chemical database) but relies on them for technical input. During 1980, Dr Lowen Garson and Stanley Cohen of ACS took one journal, *Journal of medicinal chemistry*, and made it available as a full text test file on BRS. Some 980 documents were involved (amounting to 16 megabytes of storage). Twelve leading US institutions were invited to evaluate the file. Even though the file was small and "dead" — only 1976-1978 articles were mounted — the respondents found it useful for a number of reasons. Some found that it enabled relevant paragraphs from articles to be identified, even though the separate abstract had not included the necessary key words. Some also made use of the file for full text document delivery of the required articles. On the negative side, the lack of graphics was considered a major problem by some users. Based on the evidence provided by this study, ACS plans to place all their 1980 journal issues into full text format by January 1981, as well as five years backfile of *Journal of medicinal chemistry*. Updates will be made biweekly, and will be available on the database file more quickly than the printed journal will reach some US locations. The

88

market base will be extended to a sample of 100 users who will be expected to supply more critical and detailed evaluation. The ACS full text database will not be made a public file accessible to all BRS users until all the technical "bugs" have been eliminated from the system. To some extent, ACS will be awaiting the increased adoption of "graphic display terminals" (currently costing upwards of $10,000) before launching this full text service. But the fact that 95% of all US chemists have direct access to computers, in whatever form, is considered a key ingredient for making this experiment financially viable in the long term'.[15]

Some major publishers, some institutions and societies, have therefore begun to make the adjustment to the new age. Gordon Graham, mentioned earlier, has fully committed his long-established firm, Butterworth, to electronic publishing (LEXIS, the full-text legal system described in Chapter 4, is a prime example of his commitment). Addressing the 1981 Libtrad Conference in London, he emphasized the fact that the stage of technological pioneering is over and that the new technology represents very much more than a minor change. He also pointed out that it is a big investment, big risk business. He reminded his audience – of publishers, booksellers and librarians – that traditional roles do not fit into the new world, and warned that the inheritors of this new world might not be in direct linear descent from those roles. For him, as a publisher, the likeliest future scenario lay in small specialized full-text databases, offering a direct service to users. He considered on-demand printing and document delivery services as being only interim arrangements.

Graham also referred, as many other commentators have, to the blurring of traditional roles. Like Robert Campbell, quoted earlier, he observed that the librarian is becoming a secondary publisher, a purveyor of information. He felt that printers, booksellers and librarians have to come together in the new situation. They must cooperate, not compete. Likewise there must be a change from the national to the transnational.

Professor Brian Vickery, Director of the School of Library, Archive and Information Studies at University College, London, addressing a seminar organized by the Standing Conference of National and University Libraries in London in January 1981, also commented on the wide range of interests in the information technology field: extending beyond the 'library community' into the 'information industry', embracing the whole process from the generation of information to its use. He argued that both information providers and information users needed to be re-educated in the new modes, and that the concept should be developed of an overall, coordinated information network, based on the new technology. At the moment database providers operated quite independently of the library community, and the strong commercial interests of publishers had driven them to consider even purchasing the British Library Lending Division. Addressing the same seminar, M W Hill, Chairman of the Aslib Council, accepted that all of the information field — storage, retrieval and transmission — was in a state of transition, but unlike Professor Vickery, argued against any kind of national coordination, which he considered might have the effect of ossifying the process. The problem with coordination, he pointed out, is that progress depends on the unreasonable man. Where he did see the need for a national policy was in relation to two major factors on which such progress was dependent: copyright and data protection.

Gordon Graham's reference to the big investment, and the big risks, involved in electronic publishing, is not the only problematic economic aspect of these new departures. A recent article[16] drew attention to the persistent concern of traditional abstract journal publishers as to whether the growing use of on-line databases is at the expense of subscriptions to the printed version: 'The two publishing systems operate on quite different economic bases. Ninety percent of the subscription price of a printed journal is received as upfront money by the publisher in the conventional printed system, whereas with on-line database searching, the owner of the database at best receives 25-30% of the royalty from a search, with the rest being divided between the on-line vendor, the telecommunications authority, and, if transatlantic database searching is involved, the packet-switching service. Furthermore, the money is received after the event, giving no opportunity to earn interest on prepayments'. The article goes on to quote the findings of Patrick Barwise (1979) that on-line royalty charges would have to double or treble over the next few years to provide secondary services with sufficient funds to tide them over the transitionary period before the build-up of on-line royalty income; and also to mention a more recent financial analysis by Martha Williams which pointed similarly to an increase in prices for on-line users (which could have a detrimental effect on the assumed market growth potential for database searching, especially in Europe).

L J Taylor,[17] among others, is more concerned with the sociological and political consequences of the economic change in publishing. It is all very well to accept the technological inevitablity of the datapack, telecommunications and super-intelligent terminal, and to discuss as librarians, booksellers and publishers, the future nature of publication, but as Taylor is right to warn: 'It seems to me that these developments point to the closure of traditional open publication and the establishment of groups of privileged consumers. Only the very popular material will be worth publishing in the general sense at all. Orwell's dichotomy between the proles and the party will not be so far off the mark after all, unless massive safeguards are built in to preserve equality of access to information for all'.

In fairness it is also imperative to record that — despite the obviously pre-emptive nature of the technology, despite the equally obvious and increasing failure of traditional systems to meet the current needs of our society, despite the bold ventures into and serious experiments with the new technology by major commercial and academic institutions, and despite striking successes such as the now all-pervading on-line systems — there remain many doubting Thomases. An outstanding example is to be found in the comments of A K Kent[18] on the prospects for scientific and technical publishing in the 1980s. Kent does not believe that the 1980s will see much change, and that the predominant mechanism for the transfer of scientific and technical information will continue to be print on paper, such in his opinion is the convenience and ego-enhancing qualities of the printed page. He does not think that the electronic journal will be realized in its fully computerized form. Though he is confident of a significant move away from printed abstracting and indexing publication towards on-line databases, he does not foresee a reduction in costs of access, but an increase of between three and ten times in real terms over the decade, more than eliminating any savings arising from lower computer or telecommunication costs. He forecasts a period of dangerous instability in our systems for information transfer, with a rapid increase in the cost of use of information and the collapse of some and possibly many of the established institutions and practices in the field without the compensating replacement of them by effective alternatives. He does not expect any kind of renaissance within the decade, because he believes that the mechanisms for information transfer are moving rapidly into the hands of the irresponsible, and that this unfortunate transition is being further fuelled by the accelerating application of inappropriate technology. The only hope he can see — echoing Professor Vickery, quoted earlier — would lie in a coming-together of the major creators, processors and users of information to understand each others' problems and to develop together a common strategy for advance. He observes in conclusion that if technology and the opportunity it offers for the future causes us to run before we can walk then none of us may pass the finishing line.

To return however to the future of the book as such. Many of the defences offered, while too gentlemanly or too ladylike to be out-rightly Luddite, have taken refuge in some curious strategies. Often quoted, for example, is the humorous defence *Learn with BOOK* by R J Heathorn, reproduced from *Punch*:

'The new device is known as Built-in Orderly Organized Knowledge. The makers generally call it by its initials, BOOK.

'Many advantages are claimed over the old-style learning and teach-ing aids on which most people are brought up nowadays. It has no wires, no electric circuit to break down. No connection is needed to an electricity power point. It is made entirely without mechanical parts to go wrong or need replacement.

'Anyone can use BOOK, even children, and it fits comfortably into the hands. It can be conveniently used sitting in an armchair by the fire.'

In a light vein also (though in truth written as a riposte against some of the wilder claims made for electronic media) is the following extract from an editorial by T C J Norton:[19]

'Specification for an ideal information storage and retrieval device: it should be portable, able to function in any environment, require no power supply and be immdeiately usable with no warm-up; it should have high information storage capacity and retain the information indefinitely without degradation or possibility of accidental erasure; file access should be instant and random and it should be possible to mark up, annotate or make manual corrections to text.

'There is no electronic device which meets this specification, nor is there likely to be in the foreseeable future. On the other hand, there is a non-electronic device which fully meets the specification (and more) and has done so for over 500 years. I mean, of course, the book.'

Altogether more earnest, but of an identical type, is the tabulation offered in an article called *In defence of the book* by Jenny Rowley:[20]

The book	Computer databases
1 Relatively low density of data storage	Higher density of data storage
2 Very portable, except in large numbers	Portable, but needs careful handling

92

3 Will survive most environments, although life depends on quality of paper, binding, etc	Subject to deterioration and even erasure in some environments
4 Can be read without intermediate equipment (except spectacles!)	Needs additional equipment to convert to format suitable for human reading. Ease of reading depends on this equipment and its accessibility
5 Can be read in an armchair, a desk, in the bath, or wherever convenient	Reading must be conducted in an upright sitting position at the computer terminal, unless printed text is generated. Computer terminals must be connected to other equipment and are not generally regarded as portable
6 Several can be used simultaneously and compared	Comparing two or more databases or parts thereof means flicking between two sets of text on the screen
7 Can be scanned in order to judge whatever is covered in the following few pages, and to review the plan of the book	The ease with which this can be accomplished depends on the system. Additional terminals would, naturally, facilitate readier comparison. Scanning is possible, but usually must be sequential and thus can be slow
8 Its diagrams and illustrations can be used to amplify and elucidate points	Diagrams are sometimes available with a terminal with graphic facilities, but pictures cannot be faithfully reproduced
9 Can be a work of art, with both a tactile and visual appeal	Computer terminals are distinctly limited in this respect. All efforts at improving display of text are rooted in functionality

The problem with these and similar defences of the book is not that they do not contain substantive points, but that they are based on a totally false premise. Nobody is (or should be) aiming to contrast a utilitarian visual display unit with an ordinary familiar book and claim that the first is much better than the second (though Joseph Raben did point out that the first books, chained to library walls to prevent theft, were not very cuddy either). The real contrast lies in the two systems of which each is the respective product. Behind the traditional book lies an increasingly inappropriate and inefficient information system, epitomized by our increasingly unusable libraries. Behind the visual display unit however lies the firm possibility and prospect of an efficient, convenient and fully accessible communal memory for mankind. In any case, bearing in mind A J Meadows's counsel about categories (referred to earlier in this chapter), the defenders of the book will find no difficulty in staking out at least some areas where it seems likely that the book will persist for an appreciable time.

It is salutary to remember that J C R Licklider at the very outset of his seminal 1965 study on the libraries of the future made it clear that he had 'delimited' the scope of his report to include only 'transformable information': 'Works of art are clearly beyond that scope, for they suffer even from reproduction. Works of literature are beyond it also, though not as far. Within the scope lie secondary parts of art and literature, most of history, medicine, and law, and almost all of science, technology, and the records of business and government'.

Admittedly close reading of his statement of limitation does reveal that in fact very little is excluded. A book that is a work of art — a fifteenth-century Book of Hours, say, or an Aldine press edition — will certainly never be under any threat. It is not transformable and will be preserved even in a museological sense. Licklider qualifies his own prediction about works of literature; and the present writer has qualified it further in the argument previously offered that new works of literature are likely to be written for the prevalent media of their age, and earlier works transmuted into new media forms (as *Gone with the wind* to film).

Relevant here also is a recent report[21] on the potential impact of cable television in the United States: 'In spite of the fact that the majority of cable TV networks in the US are losing money, a strong feeling exists in the publishing world that the traditional concept of a book may, in certain subject areas, be supplemented, threatened or even replaced by information entered directly into microcircuitry, thereby by-passing the book format and the multi-faceted publishing process which the latter entails. The basis of this view is the growing number of US television households with cable reception: 5% in 1968; 27.8% in 1981, with a monthly subscriber growth-rate of 250,000. According to Bill Parkhurst (*Library journal*, 220, (19), p29) by 1990 we can expect a 50% penetration that will grow to nearly 80% of American households watching cable (TV) by century's end. At present, all the talk is of the possibility of reading fictional bestsellers, writing letters, paying bills, shopping, playing chess, gambling . . . through a cable link comfortably positioned in one's own home'.

The latter part of Licklider's statement, of course — 'secondary parts of art and literature, most of history, medicine, and law, and almost all of science, technology, and the records of business and government' — in one tremendous sweep brings in the greater proportion of mankind's working memory, and leaves little comfort for those who hope to see all forms of the book persist forever.

It would though after all be very surprising if the concept of the loss of the book were to be taken lightly by anyone. As A R Turnbull observed in the radio broadcast referred to at the very beginning of the present chapter, the printed book surely ranks as man's greatest invention, one which injected a dynamism into Western society and became over the last five hundred years the great tool of education. No doubt that is one of the reasons why Gordon Graham at the 1981 Libtrad Conference maintained he saw no immediate prospect of the book becoming extinct (while at the same time declaring his publishing firm's full commitment to electronic publication). The context of his declaration was that his electronic publishing ventures were not a blunderbuss approach: in a big investment, big risk venture such as electronic publishing each approach was 'very targeted'. Likewise he argued that electronic publication is at present a *searching* tool, not a *reading* tool. Again no one in their right mind would prefer reading continuously on a current generation visual display unit to reading a well-printed book, but the assumption cannot be that improvement and modification in terms of readability will not be forthcoming eventually. In any event it has always seemed to the present writer that a 'voice-over' facility could readily be added to any electronic transmission of literary text, with the option to use either or both.

Again at the Libtrad Conference, David Brown of Pergamon, while also in his turn describing his firm's major investment in the electronic future, did not at the same time neglect the advantages of the book form (though resisting any kind of cosy nostalgia). He pointed out (as Jenny Rowley did) that the portability of the book and journal is a winner: though here it will be remembered that Jenny Rowley herself added the qualification 'except in large numbers'. Brown also returned to the point that the electronic medium is not 'user-friendly', not in the sense that it is not 'cuddly' but that one has to learn to use a remote on-line database and that to learn all of the necessary procedures takes a long time. The counter to this, as was made clear in the first chapter of the present work, is that identical charges can be levelled at large libraries of books: use has to be learned, and to learn the ins-and-outs of library procedures takes a very long time indeed.

Brown's final defence was that the new media, unlike the book, require a very sophisticated telecommunications infrastructure, and one which is certainly not possible in Third World countries. Hills[22] made the same point, though more tentatively, introducing a collection of papers on the future of the printed word: 'Since at present the printed book can reach a large audience, far larger than any of the new technologies, perhaps this is a good and legitimate use of the printed word'. It is difficult not to be sympathetic to this defence. It could also be argued however that electric reading-lamps cannot be used where there is no electricity. This does not constitute an argument for candles, as opposed to electric lamps. It is an argument for introducing electricity. The Third World argument is doubtful also. Neelameghan[23] has estimated that over 90% of the capacity for generating, communicating and utilizing information and knowledge, epsecially in the fields of science and technology, rests with a small number of technologically and industrially advanced countries (some 30 countries with over $800 per capita income and sharing 35% of the world population burden) and, therefore, developing countries (about 120 countries with less than $500 per capita income and sharing over 60% of the world population burden) have to purchase the knowledge and know-how in the form of books, periodicals, reports, patents, training, expertise and commodity imports: that is, Third World countries have operated at no less a disadvantage even in terms of the traditional information system. It might equally be argued that with the growth of satellite communication this planet will be more equitably spanned.

Professor Vickery, at the SCONUL seminar in January 1981 (referred to earlier), remarked that in his opinion we shall continue reading books, using books and storing books. The main point that he was making — that books will still exist and will still have to be stored — is not one to be denied. The 30 million unique titles printed since Gutenberg are not going to disappear. The real attack of the pre-emptive technology, as M W Hill made clear at the same seminar, will be in the area of new information, news information — not older material. Nor, as has been indicated elsewhere in the present work, will there necessarily be any systematic programme of retrospective conversion. Hill went on to say that a lot of paper has to be stored for humanistic scholarship for a long time yet. He also observed that there will still have to be a large 'underground' of paper: which is bound to be true in the sense that neither the printing-press nor the typewriter put paid to handwriting. The retention of large stores of books — static stores — is certainly part of any long-term scenario. After all, still preserved in the British Museum are the clay tablets from the library of Ashurbanipal at Nineveh.

In a private interview with the present writer Professor Vickery emphasized the immediate relevance of the new technology to data, information and research (particularly scientific monographs and journals). He also emphasized however that this kind of information, relative to the whole population, is used by very few people, and while accepting that the printed word will be less pervasive, he could not accept that the man in the street will be served via the terminal, but will turn to the book for recreational and inspirational reading.

In the short/medium term Professor Vickery may be right. The general popularity of paperbacks with the man in the street is evidenced by the very great number of commercial outlets for their purchase — not just bookshops, but newsagents, department stores and super-markets. The initial print runs for authors such as Frederick Forsyth and Harold Robbins are very large and sales for such authors in the United Kingdom can be as high as one million copies annually. The market for paperbacks, according to M S Broadbent and J D Powell of Parker's Bookstop in Oxford, in February 1981, was even weathering the general economic recession.

Broadbent and Powell also reiterated the fact that in publishing generally the annual output of new titles is still increasing. This fact has been referred to elsewhere in a printed report,[24] as a 'paradox' — more titles being published, more firms failing; and in yet another,[25] with the suggestion that publishers have decided during a difficult time of falling print runs and sales per title the only way to maintain turnover and contribute to overheads is to increase the number of titles issued.

Broadbent and Powell's forecast for the next 5 or 10 years in book-selling was optimistic. They felt that people would buy books if they had the money. There are less academic book buyers (on legs, that is), but the general book buyer has increased in number. The 'leisure' book market is increasing. Fiction (hardback) publishing is drifting off into the past. The market for multiple texts (for schools, for example) is under pressure. Publishers are not reprinting books: though Broadbent and Powell see this as an effect of the economic recession, not as a trend. Secondhand bookshops are not doing very well: business is too slow. Overall, hardback publishing is giving way to paperback publishing.

It is however difficult not to feel that the man in the street's money for entertainment and recreation — and perhaps even inspiration — must surely in due time be substantially tempted away from paperbacks and leisure books. Not only is it a statistical fact that individuals now spend more time viewing television than in any other leisure activity — including reading — but other electronic entertainment vistas are opening up all the time — cable television (as noted earlier), videorecorders (a rapidly growing market), TV games, video discs. At the popular level also, the new technology is pre-emptive.

In sum the consensus of the evidence is that the integral form of the new age will be electronic. The book at best will be no more than a partial realization of that form (the butterfly, not the chrysalis[26]). What then of libraries?

References

1 McLean, Ruari *The Thames and Hudson manual of typography.* London, 1980.

2 Raben, Joseph 'The electronic revolution and the world just around the corner' *Scholarly publishing*, 10 (3), April 1979.

3 Burchinal, Lee G 'Impact of on-line systems on national information policy' *In* Kent, Allen and Galvin, Thomas J, *eds. The on-line revolution in libraries: proceedings of the 1977 Conference in Pittsburgh, Pennsylvania.* New York, Marcel Dekker, 1978.

4 Meadows, Arthur Jack 'The future of the printed word: economic and social factors' *In* Hills, Philip, *ed. The future of the printed word: the impact and the implications of the new communications technology.* London, Frances Pinter, 1980.

5 Gates, Yuri 'A note on videodiscs' *In* Hills, Philip, *ed. The future of the printed word: the impact and the implications of the new communications technology.* London, Frances Pinter, 1980.

6 Meadows, Arthur Jack, *op. cit.*, 4.

7 Meadows, Arthur Jack *New technology developments in the communication of research during the 1980s.* Leicester, Primary Communications Research Centre, University of Leicester, 1980.

8 Cabinet Office, Advisory Council for Applied Research and Development *Information technology.* London, HMSO, 1980.

9 *Outlook on research libraries*, 3 (1), January 1981, p10.

10 *Outlook on research libraries*, 3 (4), April 1981, p2.

11 *Outlook on research libraries*, 3 (4), April 1981, p8.

12 Goldstein, Charles M *Videodisc technology and information systems* (presentation at the Third International Online Conference, London, December 1979).

13 *Outlook on research libraries*, 2 (9), September 1980, pp6-7.

14 *British Library Research and Development newsletter*, 21, September 1980, pp1-2.

15 *Outlook on research libraries*, 2 (11), November 1980, p9.

16 *Outlook on research libraries*, 3 (2), February 1981, pp6-7.

17 Taylor, L J 'Selections from a committee' *Library Association record*, 83 (1), January 1981.

18 Kent, A K 'Scientific and technical publishing in the 1980s' *In* Hills, Philip, *ed. The future of the printed word: the impact and the implications of the new communications technology*. London, Frances Pinter, 1980.

19 *State librarian*, 29 (1), March 1981, p1.

20 Rowley, Jenny 'In defence of the book' *Library Association record*, 83 (12), December 1981.

21 *Outlook on research libraries*, 3 (12), December 1981, p12.

22 Hills, Philip, *ed. The future of the printed word: the impact and the implications of the new communications technology*. London, Frances Pinter, 1980.

23 *Outlook on research libraries*, 3 (4), April 1981, p3.

24 *Library Association record*, 83 (1), January 1981, p4.

25 *Outlook on research libraries*, 3 (2), February 1981, p9.

26 Line, Maurice, B 'Some questions concerning the unprinted word' *In* Hills, Philip, *ed. The future of the printed word: the impact and the implications of the new communications technology*. London, Frances Pinter, 1980.

Chapter Six

THE END OF LIBRARIES

The end of libraries could be to adopt a museological role and see out the printed era. Billions and billions of printed words already exist and are likely to continue to exist because, as Maurice Line has observed,[1] though it will be technically possible to convert most if not all to electronic form, there would seem little point in doing so until the cost of storing and conserving them becomes much greater than the cost of conversion and subsequent access.

Every commentator on the mixed and changing future has acknowledged that it will need to include an archiving facility. Libraries have been visualized as becoming document centres; many existing books will have to be stored since retrospective conversion to electronic form will realistically be within what Verina Horsnell has referred to as 'engineering tolerances'; and as M W Hill commented, a great deal of paper for humanistic scholarship will have to be stored for a very long time yet.

If however libraries settled for no more than an archival function and succumbed entirely to the operational paralysis described in the opening chapter of the present work, then their decline would be inevitable. They would lose their basic connection with information access. They would have no recreational function, and only a very limited (and decreasing) role in education and culture. They would cease to have any social or political importance. The crux of the matter is that these vital roles and functions have for almost three thousand years constituted the central and essential tradition of libraries, as the present writer sought to demonstrate in two previous works.[2,3] Libraries have never been peripheral to society. Indeed it has been professional over-emphasis on the repository or archival function of libraries which has most worked against the fulfilment of their true tasks. This latter view has been many times enunciated, most recently and with particular relevance to the current situation by Dr Donald Urquhart:[4] 'Modern librarianship must reject collecting as an end in itself'.

It was in the 1970s 'that technology at last began to make big inroads into areas where customs and techniques had scarcely altered for decades, and provided the means to transform some long-cherished ideas into working realities'.[5] Fortunately, as Miriam A Drake has noted,[6] though for many years librarians reacted negatively to any system which altered the existing order of the library, now: 'the number of librarians who flee to the stacks when the computer terminal arrives is diminishing'. She goes on to say that in any event (and again picking up the theme of the opening chapter of the present work) librarians' attitudes to users were due for re-examination and re-formulation. 'Consumer awareness of information provision and alternative forms of information service are increasing. Librarians are slowly realizing that a book or journal is not information and that many library user needs cannot be satisfied with a list of citations or directions on how to use the catalog. Library users have changed their roles from guardians and supporters of libraries to consumers of information services. This change has been described as a shift from asking, "Where is the answer . . . ?" to "What is the answer . . . ?"'. She adds: 'Changing the focus of the library from record keeping to human users is a challenging task'.

One example of adjustment to the new task has been public library experimentation with Prestel (fully described in a previous chapter, Chapter 4). As Geoff Andrew and Verina Horsnell reported in the official journal of the Library Association,[7] initial library involvement coincided with the launch of Prestel by the Post Office in 1978. A British Library financed research study was carried out jointly by the Library Association and Aslib in six public libraries – Birmingham, Norwich, and the London Boroughs of Bexley, Hounslow, Sutton and Waltham Forest. The study aimed to assess the impact of Prestel on public library reference services, and to investigate Prestel's potential as a vehicle for conveying community information. Andrew and Horsnell commented that as a wide ranging and potentially widely usable information source, Prestel cannot be ignored by the library community. Unless librarians accept the challenge provided by Prestel to make a more up-to-date information service available to residents, somebody else – maybe without the skills, expertise and impartiality which librarians traditionally have offered – will, and the combined result will be less effective information services and 'libraries taking a further step backwards into obscurity and irrelevance'.

In respect of Prestel also, serious attention has been given to its use

101

in higher education, and therefore to its relevance in academic libraries. Norman E Willis[8] has identified the following as what Prestel can offer to education: a mass communication system which is perfect for fast-moving information; a valuable resource for course content; a sophisticated delivery system for some types of learning material; and a useful tool for training in information handling. As M Aston observed at a seminar on Prestel in higher education,[9] educationalists (among whose number academic librarians should surely count themselves) must grasp the opportunity of involvement: something they failed to do when television became a mass medium. Gillian Leary[10] has also stressed that Prestel was designed as a medium of mass communication and that 'libraries should be able to play a major role in the successful development of any new mass information system'.

On-line information systems have of course already altered some aspects of libraries. J Akeroyd and A Foster[11] noted that on-line information retrieval is now widespread throughout the United Kingdom. It was first employed in the larger special libraries, and only relatively recently have academic libraries begun to adopt it as a standard method of information provision. The short survey conducted by Akeroyd and Foster showed that 70% of academic libraries are now users. The five main reasons cited by academic libraries for introducing on-line services are reported (in order of priority) as: greater cost-effectiveness than with manual methods; greater retrieval capability in search strategy formulation; access to a much wider range of bibliographic sources than in your own library; rationalization of indexing and abstracting services would be possible; and will encourage users to carry out literature searches when they would otherwise not search manually. Akeroyd and Foster also noted that most services were directed at academic and research staff and few (unlike American academic libraries where they constitute 27% of users) at undergraduates, and that British academic libraries have marketed these services (again unlike the large academic libraries in the United States) only in a fragmentary manner. They summed up the situation (in 1979) thus: 'On-line information retrieval is certainly increasing in UK academic libraries, more so perhaps where there is an existing pattern of information provision to academic staff and students. The impetus of this growth would seem to be the several centralized services which have acted as stimulants in introducing academic establishments to on-line information retrieval. The majority are now passing through an experimental stage where they are integrating on-line retrieval into their normal information services'.

102

An example of what an enlightened British academic library can offer both in terms of videotex services and on-line services is afforded by Brunel University Library, as described by R W P Wyatt:[12] 'Ceefax and Oracle are available freely for use by enquirers. There is a Prestel terminal in a prominent position to which all library users have free access for a two hour period each day when it is heavily used, and at other times it may be viewed upon request. Nearby there is a terminal for online bibliographic searching, giving access to Dialog and Blaise databases; the most popular databases are Compendex, RAPRA Abstracts, Psychological Abstracts, and ERIC. On-line bibliographic searches are performed by three assistant librarians, and normally an assistant librarian will conduct the search in the presence of the enquirer in order to tailor the output closely to the enquirer's needs'.

In special and academic libraries the value of on-line information retrieval is readily apparent, but such provision in public libraries raised a number of questions concerning the extent to which it would fit in with existing reference services, whether the public would make use of the facility and whether there would be any overall advantages. Stella Keenan, Nick Moore and Anthony Oulton have described[13] two recent research projects, both supported by the British Library Research and Development Department, which sought answers to these questions. The first project, BIROS (Bibliographic Information Retrieval On-line Service), was an on-line service offered to the general public by the Lancashire Library. The second involved four public libraries (Birmingham, Leicestershire, Liverpool and Sheffield), was coordinated by Stella Keenan, and resulted in the production of guidelines. The overall impression gained from the two projects was that there was indeed a genuine demand for on-line services amongst the general public and that that need could be met by public libraries. Keenan, Moore and Oulton concluded that on-line information can make 'a valuable contribution in widely differing types of authority, whether urban or rural'.

The general acceptance of the value of on-line information provided by libraries was also evidenced by the introduction of POLIS (the Parliamentary On-line Information System) in the House of Commons Library in October 1980. This system enables that Library to record and retrieve references to a wide variety of parliamentary questions, some proceedings and debates, and the Papers and Bills of both the Lords and the Commons. To the system over the coming years will be added other types of information of parliamentary interest.

The Library Association itself, in a recent policy statement, strongly

103

endorsed the provision of on-line services in libraries: 'Librarians and information officers actively encourage the use of, and access to, information and are not content to remain passive curators of information resources. The potential benefits to national prosperity that can be gained from vigorous public and private information services are very real. On-line facilities provide an opportunity for developing information provision to which libraries of all types should respond'.

Underlying all of this acceptance and endorsement however is the recurrent anxiety that by its very nature the pre-emptive technology could in the end by-pass libraries. M W Hill, the Chairman of Aslib Council, at the SCONUL seminar held in January 1981, did characterize *databanks* (such as Prestel) as systems (unlike surrogate *databases*) which can be quite independent of libraries. Henry Galloway,[14] having declared that no librarian can afford to ignore Prestel, does nevertheless go on to add that 'librarians are middle-men, providing guidance and interpretation, but they are a stepping-stone Prestel does not need'.

Above all else though, there is a widespread realization that libraries have reached a watershed. This was succinctly expressed, in respect of academic libraries, by David C Weber, the Director of Libraries at Stanford University, as follows:[15] 'American academic libraries have reached a watershed that is almost as significant as the change from block printing to printing with movable type. This conclusion is based on the assumption that on-line computer-based operational programs constitute a radical and permanent change in cooperative style. When one is freed from most of the constraints of the card catalog, of the US mail, and of locally prepared cataloging data, this adoption of sophisticated on-line computer-based programs may well be by far the most significant change ever achieved in library operations. It is a permanent change in the mode of library operations which should be accomplished during the period from 1965 to 1990'.

This realization of a watershed has also been exemplified in the setting-up by OCLC's Research Department of a programme to analyse existing systems and to design and construct prototype devices for 'home information delivery'. The OCLC leaflet describing the programme states the question to which the programme as a whole addresses itself: 'What existing or innovative services can be offered to library patrons outside the physical confines of the library?' It goes on to observe that libraries are moving towards the delivery of new and traditional services to patrons via electronics and computers — home access to library catlaogues, electronic encyclopaedias, interactive cable television book discussions — and summarizes the research programme's overall aim as being to look at 'ways to promote libraries as *the* information source of choice'.

This may seem revolutionary, but — as John G Lorenz[16] remarked in the context of research libraries — in reality it is *evolutionary*. It is, he says, a process of gradual change: libraries are (pursuing his Darwinian analogy) 'really just beginning to come out of the trees'. Alphonse F Trezza, addressing the same 1977 Pittsburgh conference, also emphasized the evolutionary nature of library change, using recent library history to illustrate his thesis: 'Think back a little. After World War II, the book budgets at universities increased dramatically, but look at them today, and you will notice the tremendous shift in the amount of the book budget that is spent for journals compared to the amount that was spent years ago. You will discover that what the decision-makers decided was, as a matter of priority, to put more of the acquisitions money into journals and that meant less for books. Okay, then by following the same reasoning a library might well decide that database services are so basic, are so important, that they deserve a priority in the budget and, therefore, will be charged to the book budget and something else has to suffer for it — less monographs or journals, for example, or perhaps less staff'.

Richard De Gennaro, at the same conference, likewise resisted the concept of a revolution: 'I have been experiencing revolutions in libraries ever since I got my first job at NYPL in 1956'. Speaking in 1980[17] however De Gennaro did concede a substantial evolution: 'What is needed, and what is being developed and implemented, is a new library technology based on electronics as well as fundamental restructuring of traditional library goals, relationships, and dependencies; this restructuring will force all libraries to undergo a major transformation in the coming decade'.

Harking back to the first chapter of the present work, and again using a Darwinian analogy, a consensus view has now emerged that if libraries do not change, do not evolve, they indeed most surely face a dinosaur-type extinction. If they do change and evolve, a variety and range of prospects and scenarios have been predicted or proposed.

Professor A J Meadows[18] considers that in principle research libraries should be in a good position to cope with electronic input, since its use for information retrieval and for various in-house activities is already well tested. In practice though he can see some less favourable factors operating, and he cites as examples: '(i) many research libraries still have relatively little experience of computers; (ii) even where there has been extensive computer usage, this has often been carried out by library staff rather than by the end-user (whereas new developments may well require the end-user to play a more active role); (iii) some of the innovations are likely to by-pass the library and go directly to the office or the home'. But overall the picture he presents is as follows: 'The introduction of new technology will alter the present role of the research library. In former years, current research material was purchased for use outside the library by individual researchers: libraries were used as a back-up, especially for older or unusual (eg foreign language) material. This division has broken down, in part, because journals and monographs have become too numerous and expensive for the individual purchaser. New technology could act to help restore the former position. If so, the particular interest of research librarians will concentrate to an even greater extent than at present on the retrieval of less-common information and on mass storage ... The rapidly increasing capacity and decreasing cost of storage devices should allow research libraries to expand their holdings, especially of journal back-runs, whilst decreasing the amount of space required'.

David Brown, the Research and Development Manager of the Pergamon Press, when addressing the Libtrad Conference held in London in May 1981, also contested the likelihood of a 'Doomsday scenario' for libraries. He saw libraries remaining as a core of information, with greater access to other centres for marginal and peripheral information. He saw them fulfilling a function as 'skill centres', to access the new on-line services provided by publishers.

It is interesting to note that Meadows and Brown — neither of them librarians — firmly build into their predictions the traditional concept of a library as a storehouse: Meadows with his emphasis on the possibility of 'mass storage', and Brown with his 'core of information'. It is interesting because a growing number of librarians are looking to the eventual abandonment of this traditional principle. Lee G Burchinal, for example, at the 1977 Pittsburgh Conference mentioned earlier, referred to 'the shift from near total reliance on local holdings for answering users' needs to extensive use of outside services for accessing large, remote sources of information'. Another active proponent of this view is A Graham Mackenzie, who has declared:[19] 'It seems to me that the library's major function is to act as a switching centre for information (using the word in the widest sense to include ideas as well as hard facts), as a channel through which the user may gain contact with

106

the author's intentions and thoughts. If this is accepted as true, then it seems to matter very little whether the information is gained directly, by reaching for a book on our shelves, or indirectly, by an inter-library loan, through an electronic network, or for that matter by some hypothetical future development of telepathy — the important thing is the transmission of information, the degree of access to it, not the method'.

Certainly Burchinal's and Mackenzie's views are representative of a general trend in librarianship of recent times. Herbert S White, it will be recalled from the first chapter of the present work, justifiably derided the idea of an Alexandrian Library on every campus. There has been a long and accelerating erosion of the notion that any individual library unit could operate on an independent, self-sufficient basis. The erosion began with the setting-up of the major interlibrary loan schemes, which has now culminated in the substantial reliance of every library unit on the resources of services such as those offered by the British Library Lending Division or OCLC. Alongside these there also developed cooperative storage schemes (such as the New England Deposit Library, the Hampshire Inter-Library Center and the Mid-West Inter-Library Center established in the United States in the 1940s and 1950s) and cooperative acquisition schemes (such as America's Farmington Plan sponsored by the Association of Research Libraries in 1948). Cooperative cataloguing has a history going back to the turn of the century, with Herbert Putnam at the Library of Congress, and culminating in the MARC project, which in its turn has led to regional cooperatives such as (in the United Kingdom) BLCMP, SWALCAP and SCOLCAP. In their turn — taking SWALCAP as an example — such local consortia can process circulation (book issue) transactions cooperatively also. Thus not only is the catalogue of Reading University Library held in a computer in Bristol (80 miles away), but records of its loan transactions also. On top of all this, not only do individual libraries use schemes (such as classifications schemes) and systems devised elsewhere, but their staffs have all been trained and professionally educated on a national, not a local, basis. Only the very largest of libraries — such as the Library of Congress or the Bodleian — are able to afford any significant degree of eccentricity (in its precise meaning).

Some commentators argue however that a due acknowledgement of the interdependence of libraries should nevertheless not be allowed to lead to any situation in which the baby is thrown out with the bath water, where (to use the jargon) an 'access' strategy entirely displaces a 'holdings' strategy. P R Lewis, speaking at the Libtrad Conference, insisted that libraries would continue to function as storehouses, growing in size. He argued that a permanent, discrete store of materials will always be needed in a sophisticated world. He pointed to the fact that *national* systems of library resources are now possible. In his view the future of libraries has to be based on *permanent* sources of their own, and cannot be based on electronic data stores only.

P R Lewis though was equally quick to seek to promote the library as an agency for information retrieval: in whatever form. He characterized the value of on-line services as a way of matching the user's needs with the material published. He questioned how long printed publications such as timetables (requiring constant updating) will stand up against viewdata systems like Prestel. Addressing in particular the librarians present at the Libtrad Conference, he quoted colloquially: 'the technology is here, and relevant: if you don't use it, you're dead'.

The Education, Science and Arts Committee of the House of Commons, in its Fourth Report dated July 1980, also tried to straddle the ground between 'the vandals and the Luddites'[20] but again with its own prediction of relative emphasis: 'Each library will remain as a collection of such printed text materials and bibliographic guides as are available and judged to be most needed locally. But for most libraries — whether public, academic, industrial, governmental or other — we consider it likely that local printed holdings will meet a decreasing proportion of information demand. The library will need access to electronic bibliographic and text databases as well as to other sources of printed materials. To achieve this, it will need to acquire appropriate terminal equipment, establish appropriate telecommunication links, and develop appropriate expertise. To make the most effective and efficient use of the information network, individual libraries will need access to directories of databases and of host processors, and to catalogues of items on text databases, as well as to union lists of printed books, periodicals etc, held by other libraries'.

Scenarios more radical than merely adjusting the balance between an access as opposed to a holdings strategy have also been postulated. A leading theorist here is F W Lancaster. In 1978 he published[21] a paper entitled *Whither libraries? or, wither libraries*. The paper begins by noting that most of the solutions — including 'increased sharing of resources through networking and other cooperative activities' — commonly proffered in these times of financial, personnel and space problems in libraries, all basically still assume that 'print on paper' will continue to exist much as it has done for the past five hundred
108

years and that the library of the future will look 'only cosmetically different' from the library of today. His view (and the present writer's) is that this is not a realistic vision: indeed, it is 'myopic in the extreme'.

Lancaster's own vision of the future (which has been referred to at several points in preceding chapters) is one of a society whose formal communication will be paperless (that is, electronic). As a consequence library problems in the long term do not relate to inadequate space, or even to inadequate financial resources. They all come down to one problem only: justification for existence, simple survival. Can libraries, asks Lancaster, survive in a largely electronic world?

He began to answer his own question in *Towards paperless information systems*,[22] though not without commenting that at first sight 'one might conclude that libraries and librarians will be completely redundant when the electronic system comes into existence'. Lancaster does though believe that 'some type of library service will still be needed', and in this book (Chapter 9: *The role of the library in a paperless society*) he identifies a number of functions which libraries of the future might perform. These can be tabulated as follows:

1 Libraries will be needed to provide on-line access to resources for individuals who, for one reason or another, do not have their own terminals.

2 Libraries will be centres in which trained personnel will be available to assist the user to exploit the resources offered by databases and databanks.

3 Libraries may serve as 'printout centres' since high-speed printers may not be available to all users of terminals.

4 Libraries will continue to be chiefly responsible for the collection, cataloguing and indexing of materials of purely local or very specialized interest.

5 Libraries will play a role in making accessible to a community of users, free or at low cost, materials for which some type of fee is charged by an electronic publisher.

6 Libraries, on behalf of their users, will construct profiles of interest which can be matched at regular intervals against the characteristics of documents newly added to primary databases.

7 During the transitional period (which could be many years) between present systems and an entirely electronic world, libraries will be involved in achieving some measure of integration between the processing of printed materials and the processing of electronic materials. Some level of processing in parallel will be inevitable.

Lancaster (along with research associates Laura S Drasgow and Ellen B Marks) pursued the answer to his own question yet further at the 1979 Clinic on Library Applications of Data Processing.[23] He presented a scenario set in the year 2000, by which time in his view the rapid developments in the publishing industry (transforming the entire process by which information products are created, distributed and paid for) would have dramatically changed the face of the library profession.

Libraries in the year 2000, according to Lancaster, will with only very few exceptions offer 'multisource' catalogues. These will include not only entries for all the materials held by the network or networks to which a particular library belongs, but also entries for all externally accessible databases, primary and secondary, which any member library chooses to include. He notes that while the number of entries for 'physically owned' items will still (especially in large academic libraries with substantial quantities of older printed materials) exceed the number of entries for externally accessible sources, this ratio will gradually change as more and more becomes available through the on-line connection.

By the year 2000, he continues, libraries will have declined as institutions. In particular, library technical services will have dwindled, and the remaining library activities will have become highly service-orientated.

Academic and special libraries will allocate an increasing proportion of their budgets to the purchase of on-line access to information sources, at the expense of outright purchase. This will represent the demise of the situation (referred to in the first chapter of the present work) where libraries sought to guess or predict demand, with the result that something like 40% of the materials they acquired received no use at all. Libraries as a consequence will be smaller physically. Library staffs will also be smaller, for two reasons: first, because (as indicated earlier), technical services will have shrunk; and second, because even on the user-orientated side, more specialized information services will have passed out of the hands of libraries.

Lancaster also postulates the disappearance, in a university context, of departmental libraries, consequent upon the decline in the value of holdings of printed materials.

In library staff, generally, he forecasts a dichotomy between those handling electronic information sources, and those dealing with print and microform materials. He also sees librarians as being primarily
110

generalists: the subject specialists in the profession having become affiliated to industrial or government libraries, or operating on their own as information professionals and not affiliated to any library.

Turning to the larger public libraries, Lancaster identifies two functions which can be added to those already (1-7) tabulated:

8 Libraries will still provide books and other materials for recreation and study purposes, but will have substantially raised the level of their information service activities (a high-quality question-answering service based on a vast shared 'electronic encyclopaedia').

9 Large and medium-sized public libraries will have taken on important community information services.

In respect of (8) a gloss could be added to the effect that just as libraries even now loan, as well as books, sound recordings in disc and cassette form, the future must surely include the loan of video tapes and, in due time, video discs. Whatever else a brave future may hold, the personal financial resources of the majority of mankind are likely to remain limited. All of this is part and parcel of an inevitable 'moving the library into the home'.[24]

Another commentator who has provided a radical scenario for public libraries is Kenneth E Dowlin. In a paper entitled *The electronic eclectic library*[25] he points to the fast-growing market for home computer terminals which can access the dial-up databases, and warns that if public libraries do not soon develop a role in 'the emerging electronic revolution' they will become 'irrelevant to the people who require rapid, convenient, and energy conscious access to information and materials'. The strategy he recommends is an aggressive one: that libraries should not only seek to retain their present users, but to expand important and relevant services to a large number of new users. He too suggests some new library functions in an electronic society, the majority on the same lines as those put forward by Lancaster. One that is distinctly additional though arises from Dowlin's philosophy that just as branch libraries and mobile libraries in their time represented a breakthrough in the expansion of access, so libraries must aim for a further breakthrough based on today's communications technology. He notes the growing potential of electronic teleconferencing as an alternative to traditional communications, and therefore proposes the following function for public libraries, which may be added here to the previous tabulation:

10 Public libraries might provide computer conferencing and message centre programmes.

111

Gerald Salton, speaking at the same 1979 Clinic on Library Applications of Data Processing which considered the Lancaster scenario, did not specify further new functions which might be added to those tabulated so far, but he did point to some specific advantages a largely electronic library would have over a traditional one. First, a comprehensive machine-readable data store would eliminate the existing fragmentation of materials in a given subject over many different journals and books; second, the every-increasing volume of material would become much more manageable electronically; third, bearing in mind the spiralling economics of the present labour-intensive publishing industry, substantial savings can eventually be expected in an increasingly paperless situation; and fourth, the delays currently built into the standard publication system will be largely eliminated in an electronic system.

Finally, however, it is necessary to acknowledge that whatever scenario is proposed, whether no more than an unremitting adjustment of strategies, or a whole new departure, the process of evolution from the unusable library of the kind described in Chapter 1 to the library that can find a central place in an electronic world, is a heavy undertaking. Murray Turoff and Starr Roxanne Hiltz, also at the 1979 Clinic, provided a daunting analogy: 'The library today is a rather prominent member of the societal fleet of institutions. However, it is beginning to exhibit all the problems of the supertanker, representing a pinnacle of specialized, functional accomplishment and a singularity of purpose that may limit significantly the channels it can navigate and the forms of information it can deliver. Its inertia and size may very well make its turning radius far too large to maneuver in the storms of technological change so rapidly forming on the horizon'.

Against such a background one other question is bound to arise: what future have librarians? Some facile commentators have been quick to forecast 'the demise of librarianship'.[26] Less facilely, many commentators have pointed — especially in relation to the use of videotex systems and databanks — to the possibilities of libraries and librarians being entirely by-passed by the new technology.

More systematically, however, Professor A J Meadows[27] has drawn attention to the fact that there will be redundancies, not only due to the replacement of human beings by machines, but also because particular types of work will disappear. Overall he believes the new technology will have a de-skilling effect, allowing less trained personnel to take over from skilled labour. In his view the outcome will be that

112

librarians will face fewer problems: 'Any de-skilling implied by the introduction of electronic techniques should be balanced by the possibilities for new activities. In particular, involvement in new technology should mean that user and librarian will have to work more closely together – a development that most specialist librarians would welcome. More generally, the advent of new technology will be accompanied by a need to train personnel at all points along the communication chain. Since the technology, itself, will be evolving throughout the 1980s and beyond, up-dating and/or retraining will also be required throughout the period'.

Lancaster's view[28] is equally positive. Even if libraries in the traditional sense wither away in an electronic world, it seems to him 'rather improbable that the withering process will also affect librarians and other information specialists'. He goes so far as to add: 'Indeed, people of this background and experience may assume greatly increased importance in the future'.

His argument is that all the intellectual processing in electronic systems is conducted by humans, and that it is the intellectual processing, not the machine processing, which controls the performance of the system. It seems to him that this intellectual processing will be the responsibility of 'librarians and other types of information specialists'. He specifies 'intellectual processing' as follows '(a) the activities involved in the conceptual analysis of documents and the translation of these conceptual analyses into the terms of some limited or *controlled* vocabulary (eg a thesaurus of descriptors), a process generally referred to as *subject indexing*; (b) the transformation of requests for information into formal searching strategies consisting of descriptors, or other index terms, in specified logical relationships (the relationships of Boolean algebra); (c) the construction and maintenance of the controlled vocabulary of the system; and (d) the interaction between the information specialists in the system and the community of users, whereby these users (*requesters*) make their needs known to the system'. He spells out (d) elsewhere in his book, noting the need for people (that is, librarians) 'who know the full range of resources that are available in machine-readable form and how to obtain service from these files'. And in his year 2000 scenario (written as from that vantage point) he refers to the teaching function of these new librarians: 'Beginning in the 1980s, librarians in academic and special libraries have been extremely active in instructing members of their user communities in how to exploit on-line resources effectively. The scope of the instruction

113

encompasses search strategy, use of query languages, use of on-line resource directories, and general surveys of resources available. The instruction may be conducted on a one-to-one basis or through more formal workshops for groups. In the academic world it is now common for information professionals (on the staff of the academic library or school of information science) to present courses on information services and their exploitation within the various academic departments: physics resources for physicists, economics resources for economists, and so on'.

Perhaps though the most important of all the comments Lancaster has to make is the simple statement: 'We cannot bury our heads in the sand'. He says librarians may choose to ignore the electronic world, but that will not make it go away. It is indeed time for responsible organizations, and the library profession, to accept the implications of the new technology: for 'if we do not plan now for the years ahead, we may find the transition to be one of disruption and chaos rather than one of ordered evolutionary progress'.

One aspect of that planning has to be the training of future librarians. Professor Vickery, the Director of the School of Library Archive and Information Studies at University College, London, began a private interview with the present writer by stressing the fact that 'library schools' could no longer continue to be book-centred, and that the variety of information services is not likely to decrease. For a start therefore, he suggested that all 'library schools' need to be re-named Schools of Information Science, the latter term to include libraries and librarianship and to be broader in definition than what (especially in industrial libraries) has been called 'information science' until now. On this point it is worth noting, as confirmation of the validity of Professor Vickery's argument, that from October 1981 the Postgraduate School of Librarianship and Information Science at the University of Sheffield has been re-christened the Department of Information Studies.

Verina Horsnell, the Bibliographic and Information Systems Officer of the Library Association, again in a private interview with the present writer, expressed the view that within such a Department of Information Studies there is likely going to have to be some sort of dichotomy, some splitting of courses, between librarians/information scientists, in view of the 'mixed economy' which will obtain in the information field of the next several years. This view can again be confirmed by the example of the changes made at the University of Sheffield: within the newly named Department of Information Studies, 'the MA in Librarian-
114

ship will remain a major programme, preparing high calibre graduates for careers in the libraries of universities and other institutions of higher education, the public library service, government libraries, information services and research; the programme of study will include a strong information and information technology component'. It also links up with the retention, in the libraries of the future, of some traditional library services, as indicated earlier by Lancaster (number 8 in the tabulation, for instance). In his year 2000 prediction Lancaster comments specifically as follows: 'Education for professionals in public libraries and in school libraries has changed less than other aspects; it is a separate track in some schools, while others concentrate exclusively on the preparation of students for those branches of the profession'.

Further consideration of a 'mixed economy' situation has also been offered by Alan Gomersall,[29] but with a shift of emphasis in the argument. He observes: 'On-line searching may well have given the special librarian/information officer a new and apparently impressive skill which many see as adding dignity to his job but it is only a very small part of that job, utilized in most special libraries, if at all, for only about an hour a week. Nevertheless, the customer is, or should be, with us always, and his various needs are only met by the full range of traditional services, albeit services which now make increasing use of modern technology'. He goes on to warn those who train librarians/information officers not to be 'swayed away from fundamentals' by the (understandable) euphoria to which the new technology gives rise. To him 'the common core of user-contact at all levels, a sound knowledge of all of our stock, and a proper appreciation of both manual and mechanized retrieval is still the basis upon which our continued existence rests'.

Entrants to the Schools of Information Science of the future (and Lancaster sees them called this also) will need to have, in Verina Horsnell's opinion, a subject background. Her view is shared, particularly in respect of public libraries, by M P K Barnes, the Librarian of Westminster City Libraries. Lancaster is quite specific: information professionals will have a 'master's degree in a subject area as well as one in information science'. It is however salutary to recall at this point the views (noted in Chapter 3) of T C J Norton and S A Thornton of the Royal Aircraft Establishment Library at Farnborough, that in respect of on-line searching as such, they would rate librarianship skills higher than subject knowledge.

The syllabus of a School of Information Science, according to

Professor Vickery, should fall into two parts:

i   the structure and variety of information sources;

ii organizing access.

Lancaster, again in his year 2000 scenario, fills out this outline in more detail: 'Communication processes (formal and informal) in general, publication and dissemination processes, interpersonal communication, design and management of information services, factors affecting the effectiveness and cost-effectiveness of information services, indexing, vocabulary control, database management, information resources and how to exploit these resources effectively ("search strategy" in the broadest sense of the term), and the evaluation of information services. The librarian needs to be thoroughly familiar with a wide range of communication activities, including electronic mail systems, computer conferencing, communications networks of all types, and word-processing and text-editing systems and equipment'.

In his earlier work, *Towards paperless information systems* (1978), Lancaster expanded on 'indexing, vocabulary control', talking of the librarian's need for 'a rather thorough knowledge of indexing policies and procedures, the structure and characteristics of vocabularies used in databases, query languages'. Gomersall places similar importance on the essential disciplines of 'indexing and thesaurus control'. Where Lancaster differs from both Vickery and Gomersall — who are evenhanded in respect of all types of information source — is his insistence that the 'major emphasis' must be on 'a knowledge of machine-readable resources and how to exploit these most effectively'.

Verina Horsnell also listed 'index construction' as one of the elements in a School of Information Science syllabus, but in addition she recommended further technical emphasis: computer appreciation; 'hands on' experience; how a program works; writing programs. M P K Barnes agreed that librarians were not at present sufficiently 'technical', but like the present writer, and Lancaster, sought a wider outlook on the part of School of Information Science graduates. It would be a curious irony if the information professionals of the future turned out to be as myopic as the traditional librarian because of a fixation on techniques, on means rather than ends.

Finally, an important point made by a number of commentators — M W Hill was one such at the SCONUL seminar in January 1981 — relates to the re-training of librarians. Hill recounted how in the United States middle-aged engineers do not use calculators properly: and then

116

applied this analogy to librarians. In his view, formal re-training is perhaps required twice in our careers.

The whole question of the training of future librarians/information scientists also links with that recurrent theme in any debate on the impact of the new technology: the possibility that such 'information professionals', like information services themselves, might by-pass libraries. Professor Vickery is only one of many commentators to have asked: must the experts be library-based? The notion has even attracted its own phrase: 'the floating librarian'.

Again it was Lancaster who in *Towards paperless information systems* pointed out that there was no reason to suppose that 'librarians' would need to operate from 'libraries', since the closer society comes to a completely electronic system the less need there is to conceive libraries as physical entities bounded by walls. The 'librarian' of the year 2000, acting as a freelance information specialist, could happily operate from an office or from home. He would be 'de-institutionalized'. In his year 2000 scenario Lancaster painted in the full details: 'It seems undeniable to claim that, while the library as a collection of artifacts has declined substantially in importance in the past twenty years, the information specialist has grown considerably in stature, in recognition and in rate of compensation. This development has occurred primarily as a result of the deinstitutionalization/reinstitutionalization process. Although firms of "information consultants" and even "freelance librarians" existed much earlier, it was the 1980s before it became widely recognized and accepted that information specialists no longer needed to function within the four walls of a library — that computer terminals, in effect, gave these professionals access to vast electronic "libraries", whether they chose to work within a formal institutional environment, a private office, or from their homes. In the 1980s, then, we witnessed a veritable boom in employment opportunities for qualified information specialists outside the traditional library setting: as members of health care teams; in legal practices; as resource personnel at various levels of national, state and local government; as members of research and development teams in academia and in industry, and so on. At the same time, the rapidly increasing demand for information services led to the formation, throughout North America and Western Europe, of many new companies of information consultants. In the years since 1980 the composition of the information profession has gradually changed to the present point at which the number of individuals providing information service who are

117

not library-affiliated exceeds the number who are so affiliated'.

There is no way, writing in 1982, that the prediction in Lancaster's last sentence can be confirmed or denied. But it has been made abundantly plain, in the preceding pages, that even so there will still be many librarians operating from many libraries. These librarians in libraries will be providing skilled access to, and exploitation of, on-line information sources; they will be responsible, on a local basis, for a variety of specialized materials; they will act as essential intermediaries on behalf of individual users; they will constitute a crucial bridge during the imminent, but likely to be long drawn out, transition from a society based on the printed word to an electronic society; they will continue to loan books, and items in other formats, for recreation and study purposes; they will be foci for community information services; and they will aim, as good libraries and librarians have always aimed, to widen and expand access to knowledge. As P R Lewis remarked, 'librarianship of the database is coming': but librarianship it still is.

The overall argument has to be that the true tasks of librarians and libraries — the selection, the storage, the organization and the dissemination of information — remain what they have always been. Technological progress has produced a pre-emptive technology which in due time will displace the larger part of mankind's present book-centred communal memory. To continue to fulfil their true tasks librarians and libraries will need to evolve. It must also be borne in mind that the pressure to change is coming, not just from the potentiality of the new technology, but from the professional paralysis which has now made most of our major libraries largely unusable. In this light the new technology can only be seen as opportune, something to be grasped. The librarians and the libraries that do not accept the change will inevitably be victims of the evolution. For the dinosaurs it will indeed be the end.

References

1 Line, Maurice B 'Some questions concerning the unprinted word' *In* Hills, Philip, *ed. The future of the printed word: the impact and the implications of the new communications technology.* London, Frances Pinter, 1980.

2 Thompson, James *Library power.* London, Clive Bingley, 1974.

3 Thompson, James *A history of the principles of librarianship.* London, Clive Bingley, 1977.

4 Urquhart, Donald *The principles of librarianship.* Bardsey, Leeds, Garth, 1981.

5 Henry, W M *and others. Online searching: an introduction.* London, Butterworth, 1980.

6 Drake, Miriam A 'Impact of on-line systems on library functions' *In* Kent, Allen *and* Galvin, Thomas J, *eds. The on-line revolution in libraries: proceedings of the 1977 Conference in Pittsburgh, Pennsylvania.* New York, Marcel Dekker, 1978.

7 Andrew, Geoff *and* Horsnell, Verina 'The information source libraries cannot ignore' *Library Association record*, 82(9), September 1980.

8 Willis, Norman E 'Prestel? Never heard of it' *UC&R newsletter*, 2, November 1980.

9 *ISG news*, 14 April 1980, p6.

10 Leary, Gillian 'Vast prospects for Prestel' *Library Association record*, 83 (9) September 1981.

11 Akeroyd, J *and* Foster, A 'Online information services in UK academic libraries' *Online review*, 3 (2), 1979.

12 Wyatt, R W P 'Information services in Brunel University Library' *ISG news*, 16, December 1980.

13 Keenan, Stella, Moore, Nick, *and* Oulton, Anthony 'On-line information services in public libraries' *Journal of librarianship*, 13 (1), January 1981.

14 Galloway, Harry 'New chapter for local libraries' *The Prestel user*, 3 (3), July 1980.

15 Weber, David C 'A century of cooperative programs among academic libraries' *In* Johnson, Richard D, *ed. Libraries for teaching, libraries for research: essays for a Century.* Chicago, American Library Association, 1977.

16 Lorenz, John G 'Reaction to "Impact on library functions"' *In* Kent, Allen *and* Galvin, Thomas J, *eds. The on-line revolution in libraries: proceedings of the 1977 Conference in Pittsburgh, Pennsylvania.* New York, Marcel Dekker, 1978.

17 De Gennaro, Richard 'Research libraries enter the information age' *Library journal*, 104, November 1979.

18 Meadows, Arthur Jack *New technology developments in the communication of research during the 1980s.* Leciester, Primary Communications Research Centre, University of Leicester, 1980.

19 MacKenzie, A Graham 'Resource management in scarcity: the impact of the "new technology"' *UC&R newsletter*, 5 November 1981.

20 *Library Association record*, 83 (1), January 1981, p1.

21 Lancaster, F W 'Whither libraries? or, wither libraries' *College and research libraries*, 39 (5), September 1978.

22 Lancaster, F W *Towards paperless information systems*. New York, Academic Press, 1978.

23 Lancaster, F W, *ed. The role of the library in an electronic society: proceedings of the 1979 Clinic on Library Applications of Data Processing*. Urbana-Champaign, University of Illinois, Graduate School of Library Science, 1980.

24 *Business week*, 30 March 1981, p88.

25 Dowlin, Kenneth E 'The electronic eclectic library' *Library journal*, 105, November 1980.

26 *Library Association record*, 83 (1), January 1981, p8.

27 Meadows, Arthur Jack, *op. cit.* 18.

28 Lancaster, F W, *op. cit.* 22.

29 Gomersall, Alan 'Information work in the next decade: can the library schools provide what we will need? *In The nationwide provision and use of information*. Aslib IIS LA Joint Conference, 15-19 September 1980, Sheffield. London, Library Association, 1981.

ACKNOWLEDGMENTS

In writing this book I have sought guidance and information from many individuals. Without burdening them with any blame for the arguments offered or the facts retailed, I should like to thank the following in particular: Dr Hugh Pinnock, British Library Research and Development Department, London; Ms Verina Horsnell, Bibliographic and Information Systems Officer, Library Association, London; Professor Brian Vickery, Director, School of Library Archive and Information Studies, University College, London; Mr P R Lewis, Director General, British Library Bibliographic Services Division, London; Professor Michael Twyman, Department of Typography and Graphic Communication, University of Reading; Mr M S Broadbent and Mr J D Powell, Joint Managing Directors, Parker's Bookshop, Oxford; Mr Julian Blackwell, Blackwell's, Oxford; Mr T C J Norton and Mr S A Thornton, Royal Aircraft Establishment Library, Farnborough, Hampshire; and Mr M P K Barnes, Librarian, Westminster City Libraries, London.

J T
March 1982

INDEX

124

System Development Corporation 36, 56
Systran 71

Tait, James A 53
Taylor, L J 90-91, 99
Tedd, L A 38
Telecommunity 18
Telematics 18
Teletext 55, 63-64
Telidon 67
Thompson, James 30, 53, 118
Thornton, S A 39-40, 115,
121
TITUS 71
Tizard, Sir Henry 14-15
Toffler, Alvin 18, 30
Trezza, Alphonse 105
Turnbull, A R 76, 82, 95
Turoff, Murray 112
Twyman, Michael 67, 71, 82,
121

UKMARC 48
University Grants Committee,
Atkinson report 14, 16
Urquhart, Donald 100, 119
User education 11

Vickery, Brian 49, 89-90, 96,
97, 114, 115, 121

Video discs 55, 67-70, 82, 85,
87
VIDEO PATSEARCH 86
Videotex 55, 63
Viewdata 55, 64
Visual display units 21, 28
Voice recognition 70

Walch, David B 63, 64, 74
Weber, David C 104, 119
Webster, Wendy 59-60, 74
Westrop, Simon 66
Whatley, H A 53
White, Herbert S 13-14, 16,
107
White House Conference on
Libraries and Information
Services 23
Whitehead, John 27-29, 30
Williams, Martha 90
Williams, P W 38
Willis, Norman E 66, 74, 102
119
Wills, Gordon 11, 16, 22, 30
Word processors 27-29
Wyatt, R W P 103, 119

Xerox Corporation 68

Yale University Library 8